CATULLUS

Robert J. Ormsby, who is primarily responsible for translating from the Latin, cooperated in fashioning the translation into English verse. He is an assistant professor of Latin and Greek at Douglass College, Rutgers, The State University of New Jersey. He took a doctorate in classics at the University of Washington in Seattle.

Reney Myers, who devised the rhyme schemes and metric patterns, collaborated in shaping the translation into its present form. He is an associate professor, chairman of the Department of English at Middlesex County College in Edison, New Jersey, where he has taught calculus. He has taken an advanced degree at Rutgers University.

The two first became acquainted in 1966 when Myers enrolled as a student in Ormsby's class in Latin poetry. It was in these circumstances that they first hit upon the idea of pooling their abilities to produce this verse translation of Catullus.

CATULLUS

The Complete Poems for American Readers

Translated by

RENEY MYERS and ROBERT J. ORMSBY

Introduction by Quincy Howe, Jr.

E. P. DUTTON & CO., INC. · NEW YORK · 1970

Published simultaneously in Canada by
Clarke, Irwin & Company Limited,
Toronto and Vancouver

SBN   0-525-07815-0

Designed by The Etheredges

To Gertrude and Doris

Uxoribus carissimis

ACKNOWLEDGMENT

We wish to express our gratitude to Professor S. Palmer Bovie of the Classics Department at Douglass College, Rutgers, The State University of New Jersey, whose unfailing help and encouragement assured the completion of this work.

Robert J. Ormsby
Reney Myers

INTRODUCTION

In Roman poetry Catullus stands out as the most vivid and immediately accessible personality. His work is charged with the impulsive passion of youth: joy and grief, mordant and caustic wit, and a deep and serious veneration for the bonds of love. Yet all this passion is conveyed through some of the most finely wrought and accomplished poetry in any language. To the translator he presents an ever-renewed challenge, to the teacher he is a *vade mecum* to Latin literature that has converted many a vacillating student, and to the poet he is one who served his savage muse with an unswerving and relentless honesty.

The poetry of Catullus is of the sort that can stand entirely on its own merits. Our appreciation gains very little from biographical information, yet the poems do inevitably arouse curiosity about the poet's life. As with so many classical authors, the attempts to reconstruct the life of Catullus are based upon ambiguous information leading to questionable conclusions. Although any assembling of the facts of his life results in a web of conjecture, this has not prevented scholars from trying their hand at it again and again. The profit to be gained from this is the momentary satisfaction of bringing Catullus the man into focus. Even if the picture is only partially true, it provides a vantage point, subject of course to later correction, from which one may view the poet.

He was born in Verona in the Roman province of Cisalpine Gaul, probably in 84 B.C., although some say 87 B.C. His father was well to do and had the distinction of playing host to Julius Caesar regularly when Caesar was in Gaul. His family must also have been rather well connected with the aristocracy in Rome, for Catullus circulated among the notable and notorious of the day. One can only guess at his education. Probably he went through the usual curriculum of Greek and Latin authors, and it is very plausible that he came under the influence of Valerius Cato, one of the most powerful forces for innovation in the poetry of the age and also a resident of Cisalpine Gaul.

When Catullus had completed his basic education in Verona, he did what was expected of any young noble from the provinces—he went to Rome to seek his fortune, both poetic and amatory. He arrived in Rome perhaps around his twentieth or twenty-first year, certainly before his twenty-fifth. He seems to have fallen in effortlessly with the dissolute and frivolous intelligentsia of the day, and his poems provide a most distinguished roster of friends and associates.

Thus the opening poem of the collection is dedicated to Cornelius Nepos, the Roman biographer. Nepos already possessed a literary reputation and may very well have praised the work of Catullus. Like Catullus, he was a Gallic provincial and quite probably opened some doors to the more illustrious chambers of Roman society. One of the most infamous if not illustrious of these chambers was that of Clodia Metelli, the woman spoken of as Lesbia in the poems. She came from one of the most distinguished families of the Roman Republic and married Quintus Caecilius Metellus Celer, of equally distinguished lineage. How she met Catullus is uncertain. Metellus was proconsul in Cisalpine Gaul in 63 B.C. and probably took his wife along. Catullus may have been invited to the home of Metellus because of his membership in the local aristocracy. It is also possible that he did not meet her until he came to Rome, perhaps even, as some have conjectured in connection with poem 49, through the good offices of Cicero.

In any event, the relationship with Clodia was the most profound experience of Catullus' life and provides the immediate inspiration for many of his best poems. As a lover he deserved something better, for this woman had the loosest reputation of the day. From the poems one can adduce no less than five lovers in addition to Catullus: Egnatius (poem 37), Gellius (poem 91), Quintius (poem 82), Rufus (poem 77), and Lesbius (poem 79). This impressive catalogue accords very well with the account of Cicero, who describes her as a "two-bit Clytemnestra"—"two-bits" a reference to her cheap accessibility, and "Clytemnestra" a reference to the fact that her husband very obligingly faded out of the picture in 59 B.C. under conditions suggestive of domestic poisoning.

This Clodia, or Lesbia as Catullus calls her to shield her from the infamy of making their love public, was a beautiful and intelligent woman. The picture of her that emerges from the poems of Catullus and Cicero's speech in defense of Caelius Rufus reveals an unprincipled voluptuary, whose great pleasure it was to collect young men of fashion. She was possibly ten years older than Catullus and, at least during the early phases of their relationship, she led him to believe that she reciprocated his consuming passion. That a woman of Clodia's character and ravenous appetite would never think of giving herself entirely to a serious and permanent love relationship was something that Catullus, the callow young provincial, was perhaps too innocent to realize at first. The ardor of the opening poems (2, 3, 5, 7, and probably 51) soon gives way to distrust and misgivings. It is not long before Catullus sees that he is just one horse running in a fairly large field.

What makes much of his poetry so touching is that, even when he has incontrovertible evidence of Clodia's infidelity, he insists upon viewing his relationship with her as a sacred bond of love (cf. poem 76). In the face of the flagrant adulteries of Rome's most notorious debauchee, he goes on trying to love her *"non tantum ut vulgus amicam,/ sed pater ut gnatos diligit et generos"* (poem 72). Such an attempt is destined to failure and heartbreak, and these are precisely the straits to which this relationship reduced Catullus.

The chronology of the relationship is problematical. We know that Catullus' stay in Rome was interrupted by a one-year tour of service on the staff of Gaius Memmius, governor of Bithynia on the south shore of the Black Sea. This was probably from the spring of 57 to the spring of 56 B.C., and Catullus went off with the high hopes that had drawn many a young nobleman into provincial service—great riches from plundering the province. That he was disappointed in this hope is evident from poems 10 and 28.

Already bitter about his financial reverses in Bithynia, he was struck by tragedy, the loss of his brother, probably at the same time. Poem 101 indicates that Catullus went to the Troad, not far from Bithynia, to pay final respects to his brother, who died there. The death of his brother is also a haunting leitmotiv in poem 68. His financial lot, however, cannot have been too restrictive, for upon leaving the East, he had a yacht built for himself for the return voyage to Italy. That he had a pleasant trip back and was happy to be home is suggested by poems 46 and 31.

Upon returning from the East, he went first to his villa in Sirmio, but the city and perhaps the memory of Clodia brought him back to Rome. From this point the chronology becomes confused. It is generally assumed that he resumed relations with Clodia and that they were no more satisfying than before. To the very end he would not compromise the purity and seriousness of his feelings for her, and finally his love and tenderness turned to petulant rancor (e.g., poems 11 and 58). How and when the relationship was ended no one knows. It seems evident, however, that it created an emotional strain that was more than Catullus could bear.

This is not to say that he did not find various ways to relieve the strain. Like any young Roman, he found time for dalliance with prostitutes, as is evident from such occasional verses as poem 32. At one point, perhaps after he had given up hope with Clodia, his fancy turned to a young boy named Juventius. It is indeed pathetic to see Catullus counting kisses with Juventius (poem 48) in the same manner as once he had done with Clodia. Catullus entrusted Juventius to his friend Aurelius (poem 15). Not long thereafter (poem 24) Catullus was charging alienation of affections, as Aurelius' friend Furius had taken up intimacy with Juventius. The relationship then faded out in a series of recriminations.

Another phase of Catullus' poetic activity after his return from the East involved Julius Caesar. As the apparent successor of the democrat Marius, as a popular favorite, and as an outrageously autocratic consul in the year 59 B.C., Caesar had incurred the distrust and contempt of many of the nobles. They were appalled to see someone amass such great power by favoring the mob and bribing the aristocracy. At least as irritating as Caesar's own behavior was the rise of vulgar and greedy opportunists in his service. Such an upstart was Mamurra, Caesar's Chief of Engineers in the campaigns in Gaul. To someone well born and educated like Catullus, a person like Mamurra, apparently without background, education, or principles, living solely on his rapaciousness and Caesar's favor, was an abomination not to be endured. Catullus, disdaining even to call Mamurra by name, stigmatized him with the tag *"mentula"* or "Pricko" as he is called in this translation. This man embodied everything Catullus found offensive in Caesarism: lavish extravagance (poems 29, 41, 43, 114, 115), and indiscriminate and voracious sexual appetite (poems 29, 57, 94, 115).

Caesar, who was himself quite a dandy and very sensitive about his public, was deeply offended by the poems, according to the biographer, Suetonius. We also learn from Suetonius that Catullus later made amends for the poems, which Caesar readily accepted, inviting him to dinner on the very day of his apology. This incident suggests the incredible power of Caesar to make friends out of enemies. His most spectacular success was in winning over Scribonius Curio the younger, first a great disdainer of Caesar and then a nominal follower when Caesar paid his debts for him. By the time of his death, however, Curio was won over entirely; in Africa he went off to die for Caesar's cause in the civil war, desiring only to be remembered as Caesar's soldier. No doubt Catullus succumbed to this very same magnetism.

The circumstances of Catullus' death can only be guessed at. Tenderhearted critics and commentators are inclined to say that his disappointments in love and friendship finally proved too much for him. There are poems such as 30, 38, 73, and particularly 60 where he seems to be utterly crushed, disillusioned, and forgetful of his former happiness. His nature was mercurial and his sensibilities were delicate, which is to say that he was ill-equipped for the fast and frivolous society in which he circulated. To say that he died of a broken heart is sentimental and unwarranted; to say that he exhausted himself emotionally is borne out all too clearly by the poems.

For him the joys in life that surpassed all others were friendship and love. When he had found someone whom he trusted and esteemed, he gave unstintingly of himself. So unsuspecting a nature was bound to meet with disappointment in the circles that Catullus frequented. A provincial and an innocent at that, he threw himself at the mercy of the cool and sophisticated demimonde of the late Roman Republic. To lodge all one's trust and good faith in such jaded opportunists as Marcus Caelius, Aurelius, Juventius, or Clodia was to be blind to the realities of cosmopolitan society. Again and again Catullus' good faith was met with treachery and callousness. His poems ever fluctuate between protestations of enduring love and trust and incredulous dismay at the perfidy of his loved ones.

Catullus approached all that he did with a keen sense of piety and he expected the world to meet him on his own terms. When it failed to do so, his piety turned to rancor and spite. At times he even begged for release from the servitude that his piety had created for him (poem 76). Yet he could not change his own nature. Critics have made a plausible case for poems 30, 38, and 60 coming at the end of his life. Although the length of his life and the date of his death are both subject to dispute, there is evidence for his having lived to the age of thirty, dying in 54 B.C. In all of these late poems we see a man whose disillusionment has become unbearable. In poem 11 he gives a very apt analogue for his own life, likening his love for Clodia to that one small flower that thrives at the edge of a field, only to fall at last when grazed by the passing plough.

While living a demanding and probably dissolute life in

the very midst of a jaded and fast-living society, Catullus also managed to play an essential part in one of Rome's major literary revolutions. He belonged to a group of poets known as the *neoteroi* or "new poets." What distinguished them from their predecessors was the fact that they broke with the traditions of previous Roman poetry. Whereas the poets of the century before Catullus had been grave and public-spirited in their verse, the first century B.C. witnessed a switch from national poetry and adaptations from the Greek to an intimate and subjective poetry.

The precise origin of this "new poetry" is still a matter of scholarly controversy, but it seems to have been twofold. First and most obviously, there is in it the individual, romantic, and sentimental element of Alexandrian poetry. The most conspicuous and direct influence was exerted by Callimachus, the librarian at Alexandria from about 260 to 240 B.C. and the leading poet of his age. His verse was very tightly and meticulously structured and it bristled with learned allusions. Typical of such learning is poem 7 of Catullus, with its obscure references to Ammon, the Theban counterpart of Jove and to Battus, the legendary and equally obscure founder of the family from which Callimachus came. Typical of the finely-wrought structure is poem 68 (ll. 41–148), which has recurring themes arranged in concentric circles.

The second ingredient in the new poetry was the Roman epigram of fifty years earlier. The evidence for this is admittedly sketchy, for the epigrams survive only in fragmentary form. Among the epigrammatists were Quintus Lutatius Catulus, Valerius Aedituus, and Porcius Licinius. Their works, written in the elegiac couplet, were short and compact, usually treating some trivial or amatory subject. It is from this that Catullus got the notion of *"nugae"* or "light works," as he describes his poetry in poem 1.

These two influences—the Alexandrian form and the

Roman epigram—came together at a time when there were money and leisure at Rome to support the life of a poet. The result was the emergence of a new genre of poetry that was at once learned, personal, elaborately polished, and distinctly private rather than public. Catullus is the only poet who gives us anything by which to judge this movement, although fragments survive from his friends Calvus, Cinna, and Cornificius, as well as from Furius Bibaculus and Ticida.

Another distinctive feature of Catullus' poetry is its use of colloquialisms. When his subject matter involves banquets, napkin stealing, and the vagaries of the prostitutes' world in Rome, it obviously can gain little from the austere dignity of epic language. Therefore he turned to a poetic language that was composed to a very great extent of the vocabulary of everyday conversation. This is particularly true of the poems in the iambic meters (1 through 60).

The fact that some of his poems are light and colloquial in tone, while others like 63 through 68 are more serious in their intent, has led to the notion of a split poetic personality. Supposedly there is the light, deft, lyrical, and passionate Catullus of the short poems, working side by side with the learned and studied Catullus of the longer works. Critics have now very sensibly settled for there being only one Catullus, whose work is all of a piece, even though at one time he may be scolding a whore for her inflationary prices (poem 41) and at another writing one of the most technically brilliant compositions in the Latin language (poem 63).

What one in fact discovers is that Catullus' keen appreciation of structure and learned allusion pervades the smaller poems and that his spontaneous and impulsive passions surface throughout longer poems. The impression of multiplicity in his poetry is created by his wide range of subject matter. Almost anything can inspire him to verse of one sort or another. The poems range from the purest smut (e.g., 56 or 97) to expressions of the most tender and exquisite sensibilities, such as poem 61. Whatever the subject, there persist the same alert reactions, the same impatience with pretence and deceit, and the same willingness to think the best of those to whom he has chosen to give his love and friendship.

Another factor that has led to a fragmented view of Catullus' poetry is the order in which the poems come to us. It is evident almost at once that they are not chronological. In fact they appear to be grouped into three categories: short poems or *nugae* in varied iambic meters (1 through 60), the long poems (61 through 68), and the epigrams in elegiac couplet (69 through 116). A question that is still subject to debate is whether Catullus is responsible for this arrangement or whether the poems were so arranged by some posthumous editor. In any event, the present order presents the reader first with the lyrical Catullus, then with the learned Catullus, and finally with the epigrammatic Catullus.

Catullus' little book survived antiquity in the tenuous form of a single manuscript deriving from the tenth century and discovered in Verona, the city of his birth, in the fourteenth century. Unlike the more magisterial Vergil and Horace, he very obviously was not composing a monument for the edification of the ages. The personal lyric is not a genre that his readers looked to for instruction and information. Nevertheless he did make a sufficient impression on his own age to incur the odium of Cicero, who had little taste for poetic innovation. He had the honor of having phrases appropriated by Vergil, and in the first century A.D. he was accepted into the canon of Latin lyric poets. The epigrammatist Martial did much to revive the name of Catullus in the late first century, and then he gradually faded from view. He is mentioned by the seventh-century encyclopedist Isidore of Seville; but the first and rather incongruous evidence for the survival of his poems came from the tenth-century clergyman, Fleming Rather, who mentioned in a sermon of A.D. 965 that he had read Catullus. Again Catullus disappeared from sight, to emerge in the fourteenth century, when the Veronese manuscript of his complete poems came to light.

The study of manuscript tradition, a subject of little inherent appeal, does say something about the history of taste. The most widely read authors in antiquity were those work was public, national, or universal—a Cicero, a Vergil, or a Plato—while the literature of private life was slight and trivial by comparison. Catullus interested the ancients more for his diction and learning than for his poetry as such. It is the modern man with his interest in the particular, the personal, and the individual who has been most sensitive to the merits of Catullus.

Quincy Howe, Jr.

Scripps College

NOTE ON THE TEXT

The Latin text is chiefly the edition of R. A. B. Mynors, published in 1958 by the Oxford University Press. In several places, where the text was corrupt or doubtful, we adapted conjectural emendations from the critical apparatus of the Mynors text and the edition of E. T. Merrill, published in 1893 by the Harvard University Press.

The reader will find a glossary of proper and place names and indexes of Latin and English first lines at the back of this book.

CATULLUS

I

Cui dono lepidum nouum libellum
arida modo pumice expolitum?
Corneli, tibi: namque tu solebas
meas esse aliquid putare nugas
iam tum, cum ausus es unus Italorum
omne aeuum tribus explicare cartis
doctis, Iuppiter, et laboriosis.
quare habe tibi quidquid hoc libelli
qualecumque; quod, o patrona uirgo,
plus uno maneat perenne saeclo.

II

Passer, deliciae meae puellae,
quicum ludere, quem in sinu tenere,
cui primum digitum dare appetenti
et acris solet incitare morsus,
cum desiderio meo nitenti
carum nescio quid lubet iocari,
et solaciolum sui doloris,
credo, ut tum grauis acquiescat ardor:
tecum ludere sicut ipsa possem
et tristis animi leuare curas!

IIA

tam gratum est mihi quam ferunt puellae
pernici aureolum fuisse malum,
quod zonam soluit diu ligatam . . .

1

Who'll get my charming little book,
So freshly smoothed with pumice stone?
It's yours, Cornelius! You alone
Of the Italians, toiled and took
All time, in language learned, terse,
And dared, by Jupiter! to tell
It in three scrolls; since you thought well
Of my light works, accept this verse.
Oh virgin, muse of poetry,
Grant that it live a lifetime in man's memory.

2

Darling bird, my lover's pet,
With which, between her thighs, she plays
At war, in fingertip affrays,
When she, my love, is wont to get
An urge to feel its sharpest bites:
Why should my golden sweetheart get
This ease of longing with her pet
By pain in which her heart delights?
Oh I should like, when her desire will cease,
To let you bite me too, and give my heart some peace.

2A

It is as pleasing to me as when long ago
The golden apple pleased the fleet girl's heart, and so
She loosed her virgin's girdle, too long tied . . .

III

Lugete, o Veneres Cupidinesque,
et quantum est hominum uenustiorum:
passer mortuus est meae puellae,
passer, deliciae meae puellae,
quem plus illa oculis suis amabat.
nam mellitus erat suamque norat
ipsa tam bene quam puella matrem,
nec sese a gremio illius mouebat,
sed circumsiliens modo huc modo illuc
ad solam dominam usque pipiabat;
qui nunc it per iter tenebricosum
illuc, unde negant redire quemquam.
at uobis male sit, malae tenebrae
Orci, quae omnia bella deuoratis:
tam bellum mihi passerem abstulistis.
o factum male! o miselle passer!
tua nunc opera meae puellae
flendo turgiduli rubent ocelli.

IV

Phaselus ille, quem uidetis, hospites,
ait fuisse nauium celerrimus,
neque ullius natantis impetum trabis
nequisse praeterire, siue palmulis
opus foret uolare siue linteo.
et hoc negat minacis Hadriatici
negare litus insulasue Cycladas
Rhodumque nobilem horridamque Thraciam
Propontida trucemue Ponticum sinum,
ubi iste post phaselus antea fuit

3

Lament, oh Venus, gods of love,
And human hearts, in sorrows tried,
My sweetheart's pretty bird has died
And left her weeping here above
Who loved it more than both her eyes.
In pert affection, it would come
As she into her mother's home,
And hop about upon her thighs
And on her lap, nor did she lack
Its love song, sung to her alone.
Now far in journeys it has gone
From which no bird or man comes back;
Oh evil take you, evil death,
Who takes all creatures for your prey,
You snatched my dainty bird away.
And you, who lost your little breath,
You made my sweetheart cry today,
Her poor eyes red and sad, which had been bright and gay.

4

This boat, friends, tells us it has sailed,
Declares it flew upon the sea
And, birdlike, fled more rapidly
Than all the rest. Swift ships have failed
To catch her when they raced with oar and sheet.
All met with quick defeat.

She won the Adriatic's praise,
And praises of the Cyclades,
Of noble Rhodes, of Thracian seas,
Windy and rough, and of the bays

comata silua; nam Cytorio in iugo
loquente saepe sibilum edidit coma.
Amastri Pontica et Cytore buxifer,
tibi haec fuisse et esse cognitissima
ait phaselus: ultima ex origine
tuo stetisse dicit in cacumine,
tuo imbuisse palmulas in aequore,
et inde tot per impotentia freta
erum tulisse, laeua siue dextera
uocaret aura, siue utrumque Iuppiter
simul secundus incidisset in pedem;
neque ulla uota litoralibus deis
sibi esse facta, cum ueniret a mari
nouissimo hunc ad usque limpidum lacum.
sed haec prius fuere: nunc recondita
senet quiete seque dedicat tibi,
gemelle Castor et gemelle Castoris.

V

Viuamus, mea Lesbia, atque amemus,
rumoresque senum seueriorum
omnes unius aestimemus assis!

Of savage Pontus: she's made journeys there
When others wouldn't dare.

Before she traveled far away,
Her mast, in old Cytoris wood
Was once a stately tree and stood
And spoke in whispers, and they say
Amastris' and Cytoris' summits heard
Her softly murmured word.

The ship says these things long were known
To them, when she with rustling hair
Stood lovely on a summit there:
That she in waters madly blown
Would steep her palms, and gliding coolly by
Scorn every stormy sky.

I sailed with her and I saw how
She tacked to left and right, and knew
The winds of Jupiter which blew
Upon her sails or on her bow.
She made no vows to gods who ruled the seas,
But weathered all storms with ease.

She made her final Odyssey
To this calm lake where she will stay
And age in peace and where she may
Repose, protected from the sea.
Sacred to Castor and his twin, this ship
Has made her final trip.

(5)
Lesbia, let us live and love,
And think what crabbed old men resent,
With all their talk, not worth a cent.

soles occidere et redire possunt:
nobis cum semel occidit breuis lux,
nox est perpetua una dormienda.
da mi basia mille, deinde centum,
dein mille altera, dein secunda centum,
deinde usque altera mille, deinde centum.
dein, cum milia multa fecerimus,
conturbabimus illa, ne sciamus,
aut ne quis malus inuidere possit,
cum tantum sciat esse basiorum.

VI

Flaui, delicias tuas Catullo,
ni sint illepidae atque inelegantes,
uelles dicere nec tacere posses.
uerum nescio quid febriculosi
scorti diligis: hoc pudet fateri.
nam te non uiduas iacere noctes
nequiquam tacitum cubile clamat
sertis ac Syrio fragrans oliuo,
puluinusque peraeque et hic et ille
attritus, tremulique quassa lecti
argutatio inambulatioque.
nam nil stupra valet, nihil, tacere.
cur? non tam latera ecfututa pandas,
ni tu quid facias ineptiarum.
quare, quidquid habes boni malique,
dic nobis. uolo te ac tuos amores
ad caelum lepido uocare uersu.

The sun which sets returns above,
But once our short-lived light shall die,
In endless darkness we must lie.
So kiss me, give me a thousand kisses,
Another thousand, hundreds more,
Then hundred thousands by the score,
Confusing all men with our blisses,
So they can't cast an evil spell
Who can't keep count of kisses well.

6

Flavius, your girl must be
Unlovely, dumb, and unrefined,
Or else, old boy, you'd be inclined
To tell Catullus of your spree.
You know, I bet your slut's a mess,
Unhealthy looking, so it's clear
Shame keeps your mouth shut when I'm near;
But you don't sleep alone: confess!
Your silent bed shouts what you do:
Those pillows both indented well,
The garlands, Syrian scent's sweet smell,
Your bed's mad creaking when you screw!
No, silence won't help you a bit,
Your sagging balls reveal the lie,
You really look about to die;
You must be overdoing it.
So good or bad, tell me that I
May shout your love in merry verses to the sky.

VII

Quaeris, quot mihi basiationes
tuae, Lesbia, sint satis superque.
quam magnus numerus Libyssae harenae
lasarpiciferis iacet Cyrenis
oraclum Iouis inter aestuosi
et Batti ueteris sacrum sepulcrum;
aut quam sidera multa, cum tacet nox,
furtiuos hominum uident amores:
tam te basia multa basiare
uesano satis et super Catullo est,
quae nec pernumerare curiosi
possint nec mala fascinare lingua.

VIII

Miser Catulle, desinas ineptire,
et quod uides perisse perditum ducas.
fulsere quondam candidi tibi soles,
cum uentitabas quo puella ducebat
amata nobis quantum amabitur nulla.
ibi illa multa cum iocosa fiebant,
quae tu uolebas nec puella nolebat,
fulsere uere candidi tibi soles.
nunc iam illa non uolt: tu quoque inpotens, noli,
nec quae fugit sectare, nec miser uiue,
sed obstinata mente perfer, obdura.
uale, puella. iam Catullus obdurat,
nec te requiret nec rogabit inuitam.
at tu dolebis, cum rogaberis nulla.
scelesta, uae te, quae tibi manet uita?
quis nunc te adibit? cui uideberis bella?

7

Lesbia, how many kisses are,
You ask of me, enough and more:
As all the sands upon the shore
Of Libyan wastes which stretch so far
From Ammon's heat-seared, shimmering shrine
To ancient Battus' sacred tomb;
As all the stars which mutely shine
On furtive lovers in night's gloom.
Enough and more, such kisses will
Drive your Catullus raving mad;
But none can then count what we've had
Of kisses, nor can wish us ill.

8

Wretched Catullus, leave off playing the fool:
Give up as lost what is forever past.
But once, bright, golden suns beamed down and cast
A happiness on you when she would rule
Your steps and lead you into joyous play.
How much you loved her! More than any man
Can ever love. With her, what joy began!
That sunny world seemed yours in every way.
Yet now she does not want you, and alas,
You must not chase her nor live wretchedly,
Thus make your heart as hard as it can be. revenge?
So good-bye, baby! Catullus now will pass
You up, won't need you, nor will entertain
A thought of you nor seek your company.
Oh wicked thing, I'm tough as I can be!
Now who'll invite you? Where will you obtain

quem nunc amabis? cuius esse diceris?
quem basiabis? cui labella mordebis?
at tu, Catulle, destinatus obdura.

IX

Verani, omnibus e meis amicis
antistans mihi milibus trecentis,
uenistine domum ad tuos penates
fratresque unanimos anumque matrem?
uenisti. o mihi nuntii beati!
uisam te incolumem audiamque Hiberum
narrantem loca, facta, nationes,
ut mos est tuus, applicansque collum
iucundum os oculosque suauiabor.
o quantum est hominum beatiorum,
quid me laetius est beatiusue?

X

Varus me meus ad suos amores
uisum duxerat e foro otiosum,
scortillum, ut mihi tum repente uisum est,
non sane illepidum neque inuenustum.
huc ut uenimus, incidere nobis
sermones uarii, in quibus, quid esset
iam Bithynia, quo modo se haberet,
et quonam mihi profuisset aere.
respondi id quod erat, nihil neque ipsis
nec praetoribus esse nec cohorti,
cur quisquam caput unctius referret,
praesertim quibus esset irrumator

Praise of your beauty? Who'll make sorrows blisses?
Who'll love you now? Or bite your lips in kisses?
Not Catullus! He's determined to abstain.

9

Veranius, of all those dear to me,
Three hundred thousand, you're the very best.
Have you returned at last to take your rest
Surrounded by your happy family?
Good news! You're safe and sound! I'll hear you tell
Strange tales of far-off Spain, and what befell
My friend, whom I'll embrace so joyfully,
Whose mouth and beaming eyes my lips will press,
Oh, what other man can know such happiness?

10

Varus led me, bored, to see
His girl friend, to my jaded view,
A slut, but cute and charming too,
And having met, we talked, we three,
About Bithynia that day,
And what success my trip there had.
I told the truth, said, "Pretty bad,"
No governor could make it pay,
And none of us had come back rich;
Our chief grabbed all he could and left
The rest of us to rot. That's theft!
"We heard you did all right," to which

praetor, nec faceret pili cohortem.
"at certe tamen," inquiunt "quod illic
natum dicitur esse, comparasti
ad lecticam homines." ego, ut puellae
unum me facerem beatiorem,
"non" inquam "mihi tam fuit maligne,
ut, prouincia quod mala incidisset,
non possem octo homines parare rectos."
at mi nullus erat nec hic neque illic,
fractum qui ueteris pedem grabati
in collo sibi collocare posset.
hic illa, ut decuit cinaediorem,
"quaeso," inquit "mihi, mi Catulle, paulum
istos commoda: nam uolo ad Serapim
deferri." "mane," inquii puellae,
"istud quod modo dixeram me habere,
fugit me ratio: meus sodalis—
Cinna est Gaius,—is sibi parauit.
uerum, utrum illius an mei, quid ad me?
utor tam bene quam mihi pararim.
sed tu insulsa male et molesta uiuis,
per quam non licet esse neglegentem."

XI

Furi et Aureli, comites Catulli,
siue in extremos penetrabit Indos,
litus ut longe resonante Eoa
    tunditur unda,
siue in Hyrcanos Arabasue molles,
seu Sagas sagittiferosue Parthos,
siue quae septemgeminus colorat
    aequora Nilus,

I didn't want to say I'm broke,
And when she said, "I heard you got
Some litter bearers" I could not
Say no, and took it as a joke,
And said, "My luck was rather good,
I got eight men whose backs were straight."
Truth is, there wasn't one whom fate
Gave strength to lift a scrap of wood.
Then this bitch said, "Catullus, please,
I want to have my fortune told
By gypsies. If I'm not too bold,"
She grinned, "Will you now lend me these
Bearers to carry me?" Said I,
"Now wait. What I just meant—I mean—
What did I say? I've always been
Friends with Cinna. There's a guy,
That fellow lends me all he's got.
It makes no difference, his or mine,
It's all the same and suits him fine,
It's just as if I'd bought the lot.
But you're a slut to make a guy look small;
Nobody needles me like that, no one at all."

11'

Furius, Aurelius, companions of Catullus,
Who'd speed with him to India if he should ever go
Where distant eastern shores resound as great tides in their flow
    Rise up and fall,
Or else to soft Arabia, Hyrcania, or else
To Scythia, the archer land of Parthia, or south
To seas which Nile tints when from that great seven channeled
      mouth
    Its waters crawl,

siue trans altas gradietur Alpes,
Caesaris uisens monimenta magni,
Gallicum Rhenum horribile aequor ulti-
    mosque Britannos,
omnia haec, quaecumque feret uoluntas
caelitum, temptare simul parati,
pauca nuntiate meae puellae
    non bona dicta.
cum suis uiuat ualeatque moechis,
quos simul complexa tenet trecentos,
nullum amans uere, sed identidem omnium
    ilia rumpens;
nec meum respectet, ut ante, amorem,
qui illius culpa cecidit uelut prati
ultimi flos, praetereunte postquam
    tactus aratro est.

XII

Marrucine Asini, manu sinistra
non belle uteris: in ioco atque uino
tollis lintea neglegentiorum.
hoc salsum esse putas? fugit te, inepte:
quamuis sordida res et inuenusta est.
non credis mihi? crede Pollioni
fratri, qui tua furta uel talento
mutari uelit: est enim leporum
differtus puer ac facetiarum.
quare aut hendecasyllabos trecentos
exspecta, aut mihi linteum remitte,
quod me non mouet aestimatione,

Or if he crossed the lofty Alps and traveled where, before,
Great Caesar left reminders of the world which he describes:
The Gallic Rhine or distant Britain's terrifying tribes,
    So fierce and tall;
Thus anywhere the gods may will, however far it is,
The two of you would always be companions where I go:
So go and take these words for me to her whom we all know,
    They're filled with gall.
Tell her farewell, and may she thrive with her adulterers,
Three-hundred strong, whom she enfolds at once in her
        embrace,
Not loving one, she screws with all and never slows her pace,
    But busts their balls;
Nor can she hope to gain my love as she did once before,
Which, by her sins, has drooped and died, and so will never
        mend,
As the one flower that seemed so safe at the far meadow's end,
    Which, plough touched, falls.

12

Asinius, your thievish hands
Do not go well with jokes and wine;
Does napkin stealing seem to shine
As wit? Such conduct only brands
You dunce. But what obnoxious ways!
Am I then wrong? Just ask your brother;
Pollio wished any other
Guy had done it. He would raise
A thousand bucks to teach you sense;
He's smart. I tell you, give them back,
Or I will put you on the rack:
You'll richly earn, by your offense,

uerum est mnemosynum mei sodalis.
nam sudaria Saetaba ex Hiberis
miserunt mihi muneri Fabullus
et Veranius: haec amem necesse est
ut Veraniolum meum et Fabullum.

XIII

Cenabis bene, mi Fabulle, apud me
paucis, si tibi di fauent, diebus,
si tecum attuleris bonam atque magnam
cenam, non sine candida puella
et uino et sale et omnibus cachinnis.
haec si, inquam, attuleris, uenuste noster,
cenabis bene; nam tui Catulli
plenus sacculus est aranearum.
sed contra accipies meros amores
seu quid suauius elegantiusue est:
nam unguentum dabo, quod meae puellae
donarunt Veneres Cupidinesque,
quod tu cum olfacies, deos rogabis,
totum ut te faciant, Fabulle, nasum.

Three hundred verses, even though
The napkins have no value. They
Are gifts from friends in Spain and say,
"From farthest Saetabis, hello."
  Fabullus and Veranius are two
  Whose gifts I love and cherish as I do
  Veranius and my Fabullus too.

13

Fabullus, you'll dine well with me,
The gods approving, if you say
You'll bring the eats, and by the way,
I mean the best, and bring a free
And easy broad, with wine and wit
To salt the food, and if you do,
Then, pal, we'll live. I'm telling you
Catullus' purse is flat! Damn it
I'm broke! But on the other hand,
I'll give you undiluted love;
It's a potent perfume which
Has blandishments you'll not withstand,
It's sure to make your nostrils twitch.
My sweetheart got it from above,
From Cupid's hands, and I propose
You'll wish you were just one enormous nose.

XIV

Ni te plus oculis meis amarem,
iucundissime Calue, munere isto
odissem te odio Vatiniano:
nam quid feci ego quidue sum locutus,
cur me tot male perderes poetis?
isti di mala multa dent clienti,
qui tantum tibi misit impiorum.
quod si, ut suspicor, hoc nouum ac repertum
munus dat tibi Sulla litterator,
non est mi male, sed bene ac beate,
quod non dispereunt tui labores.
di magni, horribilem et sacrum libellum!
quem tu scilicet ad tuum Catullum
misti, continuo ut die periret,
Saturnalibus, optimo dierum!
non non hoc tibi, false, sic abibit.
nam, si luxerit, ad librariorum
curram scrinia, Caesios, Aquinos,
Suffenum, omnia colligam uenena,
ac te his suppliciis remunerabor.
uos hinc interea ualete abite
illuc, unde malum pedem attulistis,
saecli incommoda, pessimi poetae.

XIVA

Si qui forte mearum ineptiarum
lectores eritis manusque uestras
non horrebitis admouere nobis . . .

14

Calvus, I love you as my eyes,
Though I should hate you otherwise
As our Vatinius; that prize
Would send such gifts. What did I do
Or say, in innocence, that you
Should rack me with your wretched crew
Of poets? Now may heaven rain
Down every plague on him again,
Your client, who sent you that train
Of rogues, but then if, as I guess,
They're sent by teacher, Sulla, yes,
He must have sent his pupils' mess!
Great gods! What an accursed way
To stun Catullus on the day
Of Saturn's feast—no, no, you gay
Old fox, you'll never get away
With tricks like that! Let morning come
And I'll be off at once to some
Book jockey, but out every bum
Of poetry, the Caesii,
Suffenus, yes the Aquini;
Their verses will be bought by me
And sent to you; it's only fair.
Meanwhile, our age's foulest crew,
You worst of poets, go back where
Some devil fixed your crooked feet on you.

14A

If, by chance, you stop to read
The nonsense that comes forth from me,
Nor shrink from touching it with hands . . .

XV

Commendo tibi me ac meos amores,
Aureli. ueniam peto pudentem,
ut, si quicquam animo tuo cupisti,
quod castum expeteres et integellum,
conserues puerum mihi pudice,
non dico a populo—nihil ueremur
istos, qui in platea modo huc modo illuc
in re praetereunt sua occupati,—
uerum a te metuo tuoque pene
infesto pueris bonis malisque.
quem tu qua lubet, ut lubet, moueto
quantum uis, ubi erit foris paratum:
hunc unum excipio, ut puto, pudenter.
quod si te mala mens furorque uecors
in tantam impulerit, sceleste, culpam,
ut nostrum insidiis caput lacessas,
a tum te miserum malique fati!
quem attractis pedibus patente porta
percurrent raphanique mugilesque.

XVI

Pedicabo ego uos et irrumabo,
Aureli pathice et cinaede Furi,
qui me ex uersiculis meis putastis,
quod sunt molliculi, parum pudicum.
nam castum esse decet pium poetam
ipsum, uersiculos nihil necesse est;
qui tum denique habent salem ac leporem,
si sunt molliculi ac parum pudici,
et quod pruriat incitare possunt,

15

I entrust my love, Aurelius, to you,
And also my own self: I beg you, do
Me a favor. If you've ever burned
For anyone whose purity concerned
Your better side, then let this boy stay chaste.
I have no fear of those who pass in haste,
This way and that; they are the senseless mob,
Busy in their affairs; no, you're the slob
Who worries me, yes, you and your damn prick,
A threat to boys both good and bad; you stick
It everywhere. Well, use it as you like
Outside your house; screw everyone alike,
But leave this boy alone! Don't touch a hair
Of his, for if you harm the kid, I swear,
I'll fix your wagon for your treachery,
And you'll get yours, you bastard, wait and see;
When you are thrown by force into the street
For all your rotten ways, dragged by your feet,
Your ass hole crammed with radishes and fish,
You'll find it doesn't pay to sample every dish.

16

I'll fuck you both right up the ass,
Gay Furius, Aurelius,
For saying I'm not chaste, what brass!
Because my poems aren't. Thus
You miss the point; my poetry
Is simply not the same as me.
But all my verses really owe
Their wit and charm and all their salt
To spicy, merry, sexy flow

non dico pueris, sed his pilosis
qui duros nequeunt mouere lumbos.
uos, quod milia multa basiorum
legistis, male me marem putatis?
pedicabo ego uos et irrumabo.

XVII

O Colonia, quae cupis ponte ludere longo,
et salire paratum habes, sed uereris inepta
crura ponticuli assulis stantis in rediuiuis,
ne supinus eat cauaque in palude recumbat:
sic tibi bonus ex tua pons libidine fiat,
in quo uel Salisubsili sacra suscipiantur,
munus hoc mihi maximi da, Colonia, risus.
quendam municipem meum de tuo uolo ponte
ire praecipitem in lutum per caputque pedesque,
uerum totius ut lacus putidaeque paludis
liuidissima maximeque est profunda uorago.
insulsissimus est homo, nec sapit pueri instar
bimuli tremula patris dormientis in ulna.
cui cum sit uiridissimo nupta flore puella
et puella tenellulo delicatior haedo,
adseruanda nigerrimis diligentius uuis,
ludere hanc sinit ut lubet, nec pili facit uni,
nec se subleuat ex sua parte, sed uelut alnus
in fossa Liguri iacet suppernata securi,
tantundem omnia sentiens quam si nulla sit usquam;
talis iste meus stupor nil uidet, nihil audit,
ipse qui sit, utrum sit an non sit, id quoque nescit.
nunc eum uolo de tuo ponte mittere pronum,

Of words that even stir up halt
And hairy granddads—no young crew—
Whose stiffened loins can hardly screw.
Well, read my poems: If your brass
Insists my verse makes me like you,
I'll fuck you both right up the ass.

17

Colonia, what games you'd like to play
Upon your shaky bridge, but if you dance,
Its weak supports may all collapse, give way
And tumble you flat in mud as you advance.
I hope you build a longer, stronger span,
So sturdy it will hold the rites of Mars,
If you will let me laugh, laugh all I can,
When my old neighbor on your bridge sees stars
And tumbles headlong off, and in this plight
Flounders and puffs in brimming, stinking muck,
Right in the deepest hole. He needs that fright
Because this awful ass, this stupid cluck
Is lacking in the sense a two-year-old
Should have, asleep in daddy's aged arms:
He's married to a gal you should behold,
Who needs more care for her ten million charms
Than newborn kids or ripe and purple grapes;
But like a log within a waterway
He's prone, untroubled, and just sits and gapes,
Forbids her nothing; he seems made of clay,
Or just lacks all existence, he's so dense;
But if he suddenly is flung headfirst
Right off your bridge, the shock may teach him sense,

si pote stolidum repente excitare ueternum,
et supinum animum in graui derelinquere caeno,
ferream ut soleam tenaci in uoragine mula.

XXI

Aureli, pater esuritionum,
non harum modo, sed quot aut fuerunt
aut sunt aut aliis erunt in annis,
pedicare cupis meos amores.
nec clam: nam simul es, iocaris una,
haerens ad latus omnia experiris.
frustra: nam insidias mihi instruentem
tangam te prior irrumatione.
atque id si faceres satur, tacerem:
nunc ipsum id doleo, quod esurire
ah me me puer et sitire discet.
quare desine, dum licet pudico,
ne finem facias, sed irrumatus.

XXII

Suffenus iste, Vare, quem probe nosti,
homo est uenustus et dicax et urbanus,
idemque longe plurimos facit uersus.
puto esse ego illi milia aut decem aut plura
perscripta, nec sic ut fit in palimpsesto

May rouse him from his nature at its worst,
And wake him, make him shake off slothful muck
In which, like worn-out mule shoes, he is stuck.

21 *

Aurelius, starvation's endless source
Of hunger, past, and present, and to come,
You've thrust your lean desire on me, become
My love's seducer, showing no remorse,
Nor shame; you joke together openly,
And clinging to his side, you laugh and try
All sorts of things, and think you're pretty sly,
But they won't work; for all your treachery,
I'll screw you first. I'm sorry for the boy,
Whoever shares your board's half starved, like you.
In your starvation diet there are few
Mouthfuls of nourishment which he'll enjoy.
So stop, I warn you! vile and filthy crumb,
Or else you'll feel my prick in your tight bum.

22

Varus, you who know Suffenus well
Have found him gay and witty. You can tell
He's gently bred. He also writes more verse
Than anyone and also writes it worse.
Ten thousand poems, even more, are done,

* Early editors inserted a poetic fragment and two complete poems
into the Catullan corpus; these were numbered, respectively, XVIII,
XIX, and XX. Later scholars rejected these interpolations as spurious,
but by then the numbering of the poems had become traditional.

relata: cartae regiae, noui libri,
noui umbilici, lora rubra membranae,
derecta plumbo et pumice omnia aequata.
haec cum legas tu, bellus ille et urbanus
Suffenus unus caprimulgus aut fossor
rursus uidetur: tantum abhorret ac mutat.
hoc quid putemus esse? qui modo scurra
aut si quid hac re scitius uidebatur,
idem infaceto est infacetior rure,
simul poemata attigit, neque idem umquam
aeque est beatus ac poema cum scribit:
tam gaudet in se tamque se ipse miratur.
nimirum idem omnes fallimur, neque est quisquam
quem non in aliqua re uidere Suffenum
possis. suus cuique attributus est error;
sed non uidemus manticae quod in tergo est.

XXIII

Furi, cui neque seruus est neque arca
nec cimex neque araneus neque ignis,
uerum est et pater et nouerca, quorum
dentes uel silicem comesse possunt,
est pulcre tibi cum tuo parente
et cum coniuge lignea parentis.
nec mirum: bene nam ualetis omnes,
pulcre concoquitis, nihil timetis,
non incendia, non graues ruinas,
non furta impia, non dolos ueneni,
non casus alios periculorum.
atqui corpora sicciora cornu
aut siquid magis aridum est habetis

And not on scraps; his work is well begun
On royal sheets, new rolls, new bosses, ties
Of scarlet, parchment wrappers for his prize,
All ruled with lead and smoothed with pumice stone:
They're gorgeous till you read them, then you groan.
Suffenus, who had seemed so well bred, thus
Becomes a smelly goatherd. All of us,
We stare at him who just now was a wit,
Who seemed a man of letters, every bit:
He's nothing but a clumsy country lout
When he plays poet; and when he's about
To write a poem, there's a happy lad:
Delighted with himself, he's so damn bad!
Yet just like him, we all lay eggs. It's true
We're all Suffenus in a way or two;
All have illusions. We don't see the stacks
Of junk we carry, piled upon our backs.

23

Furius, you are destitute
Of servant, safe, or bed, or roof,
Or fire, but then your dad's a beaut
And so's his wife. Their teeth are proof
Against the hardest flint. You know
You're lucky he and that old goof,
Your mother, are so well, although
I'm not surprised. You'd digest rock,
And need fear nothing here below,
Not fires, thieving, or the shock
Of homes collapsing, or the friend
Who slips you poison. Thus you mock
Misfortune—you're the living end!

sole et frigore et esuritione.
quare non tibi sit bene ac beate?
a te sudor abest, abest saliua,
mucusque et mala pituita nasi.
hanc ad munditiem adde mundiorem,
quod culus tibi purior salillo est,
nec toto decies cacas in anno;
atque id durius est faba et lapillis,
quod tu si manibus teras fricesque,
non umquam digitum inquinare posses.
haec tu commoda tam beata, Furi,
noli spernere nec putare parui,
et sestertia quae soles precari
centum desine: nam sat es beatus.

XXIV

O qui flosculus es Iuuentiorum,
non horum modo, sed quot aut fuerunt
aut posthac aliis erunt in annis,
mallem diuitias Midae dedisses
isti, cui neque seruus est neque arca,
quam sic te sineres ab illo amari.
"qui? non est homo bellus?" inquies. est:
sed bello huic neque seruus est neque arca.
hoc tu quam lubet abice eleuaque:
nec seruum tamen ille habet neque arcam.

You're dry as any bone, I bet,
Or even drier; gods who send
You roasting, freezing, starving, set
You up. Why shouldn't you be well?
Like stones, you're free of spit, snot, sweat,
Their absence gives you perfect smell.
But you're still better: take your ass,
Ten shits a year and hard as hell,
The turds like beans or rocks, en masse
You rub them yet your hands stay dry,
Your fingers spotless and first class.
My god! You've reached good fortune's peak,
Why borrow dough? Let me persuade
You not to spoil your lucky streak,
For Furius, you've got it made!

24

Juventius, most tender bud of youth
Of all your clan, past, present, and to come,
I wish that you (I speak the naked truth)
Would give the wealth of Midas, one lump sum,
Instead of your love, to him who's destitute
Of servant, bank account, or bed, or roof.
You say, "But he's so handsome"; well, I've proof
That he has neither bank account nor roof;
I tell you though you may not give a hoot,
He's still without a bank account or roof.

XXV

Cinaede Thalle, mollior cuniculi capillo
uel anseris medullula uel imula auricilla
uel pene languido senis situque araneoso,
idemque, Thalle, turbida rapacior procella,
cum diua mulier aries ostendit oscitantes,
remitte pallium mihi meum, quod inuolasti,
sudariumque Saetabum catagraphosque Thynos,
inepte, quae palam soles habere tamquam auita.
quae nunc tuis ab unguibus reglutina et remitte,
ne laneum latusculum manusque mollicellas
inusta turpiter tibi flagella conscribillent,
et insolenter aestues, uelut minuta magno
deprensa nauis in mari, uesaniente uento.

XXVI

Furi, uillula uestra non ad Austri
flatus opposita est neque ad Fauoni
nec saeui Boreae aut Apheliotae,
uerum ad milia quindecim et ducentos.
o uentum horribilem atque pestilentem!

XXVII

Minister uetuli puer Falerni
inger mi calices amariores,
ut lex Postumiae iubet magistrae
ebrioso acino ebriosioris.
at uos quo lubet hinc abite, lymphae,
uini pernicies, et ad seueros
migrate. hic merus est Thyonianus.

25

Thallus, you are soft as rabbit's fur,
As goose's down, you fag, as earlobes too,
Or spider webs, or languid pricks that stir
And faint on weak old men, too limp to screw,
Yet when you're fucking you can raise more hell
Than hurricanes that scour the screaming skies:
Now look, send back that coat you stole, I tell
You it's mine; the napkin, damn your eyes,
From Saetabis, just pry it from your claws,
And tablets from Bithynia you show
Like heirlooms, or I'll flay your thieving paws
And tender ass with scourges; you will throw
Your butt about and heave, a tiny ship
Which raging winds and waters toss and whip.

26

Furius, your small estate
Has felt no winds, north, south, or west:
The hurricane that seals its fate
Is fifteen grand, to inundate
And blow apart your mortgaged nest.

27

Young steward of the choicest wine,
Bring me an undiluted cup,
Postumia says to set 'em up,
She's filled with juices of the vine.
Water, good-bye! you spoil this dew:
Go look for those who thrive on you,
Thyonian vintage suits me fine.

XXVIII

Pisonis comites, cohors inanis,
aptis sarcinulis et expeditis,
Verani optime tuque mi Fabulle,
quid rerum geritis? satisne cum isto
uappa frigoraque et famem tulistis?
ecquidnam in tabulis patet lucelli
expensum, ut mihi, qui meum secutus
praetorem refero datum lucello?
o Memmi, bene me ac diu supinum
tota ista trabe lentus irrumasti.
sed, quantum uideo, pari fuistis
casu: nam nihilo minore uerpa
farti estis. pete nobiles amicos!
at uobis mala multa di deaeque
dent, opprobria Romuli Remique.

XXIX

Quis hoc potest uidere, quis potest pati,
nisi impudicus et uorax et aleo,
Mamurram habere quod Comata Gallia
habebat ante et ultima Britannia?
cinaede Romule, haec uidebis et feres?
et ille nunc superbus et superfluens
perambulabit omnium cubilia,
ut albulus columbus aut Adoneus?
cinaede Romule, haec uidebis et feres?
es impudicus et uorax et aleo.
eone nomine, imperator unice,
fuisti in ultima occidentis insula,
ut ista uestra diffututa mentula

28

Squads of Piso, need deploys
You; baggage lightly, tightly packed;
Veranius, you've bivouacked,
Fabullus too; how are you boys?
And have you starved for lack of bread,
And frozen with that knucklehead?
Did your investment pay like mine,
Which, when I had been tricked and bled,
Left all my records in the red?
(Memmius, you laid me supine
And fucked me well, you filthy prick)
I see, boys, you too felt a dick
When looking for those high class friends!
May gods and goddesses repay
Those scoundrels for their crimes, and may
Those blots on Roman honor make amends.

29

What man can see all this and bear it too?
Only a greedy gambler, full of lust
Could stand Mamurra's gobbling as his due
What long-haired Gaul once had, and think it just
To see him drain the wealth of Britain too.
Oh faggy Romulus, can you bear this?
And if in his great wealth, he'll grin and stride
To all our beds to sniff and do amiss,
A white dove, an Adonis in his pride,
Gay Romulus, you too, then, are remiss,
A greedy lecher. And for this today,
Your gains, great marshal, in that western land,
Are gone! That fucking prick pissed them away,

ducenties comesset aut trecenties?
quid est alid sinistra liberalitas?
parum expatrauit an parum elluatus est?
paterna prima lancinata sunt bona,
secunda praeda Pontica, inde tertia
Hibera, quam scit amnis aurifer Tagus:
nunc Galliae timetur et Britanniae.
quid hunc malum fouetis? aut quid hic potest
nisi uncta deuorare patrimonia?
eone nomine urbis opulentissimae
socer generque, perdidistis omnia?

XXX

Alfene immemor atque unanimis false sodalibus,
iam te nil miseret, dure, tui dulcis amiculi?
iam me prodere, iam non dubitas fallere, perfide?
nec facta impia fallacum hominum caelicolis placent.
quae tu neglegis ac me miserum deseris in malis.
eheu quid faciant, dic, homines cuiue habeant fidem?
certe tute iubebas animam tradere, inique, me
inducens in amorem, quasi tuta omnia mi forent.
idem nunc retrahis te ac tua dicta omnia factaque
uentos irrita ferre ac nebulas aerias sinis.
si tu oblitus es, at di meminerunt, meminit Fides,
quae te ut paeniteat postmodo facti faciet tui.

So many hundred thousands! That's the grand
Result of bribes and gifts you sent astray.
Did he raise too much hell and blow his pile?
First what his father left, he spent or sold,
And then the Pontic loot he got by guile,
And thirdly Spain, where Tagus flows with gold,
And now it's Gaul, and with it, Britain's isle:
What fox is this whom you maintain? Can he
Do anything but swallow loot and steal?
That father, son-in-law both seem to be
The curse of Rome's great wealth; they wheel and deal,
And squandering all, leave ruins and debris.

30

Alfenus, false, ungrateful to your friends,
Do you now lie, deceive me for base ends?
Do you not shrink, you scoundrel, from such ways?
Bad deeds don't please the gods. You think it pays
To be deceitful, or it makes you glad,
Or you don't care, and leave me troubled, sad;
Hell, what shall I do, can I trust anyone?
I placed my utmost faith in you, for none
Urged such a love; but now your deeds betray
Me, and the pure winds blow your words away.
Though you forget, the gods remember all,
Faith too, who'll make you sorry for your heartless gall.

XXXI

Paene insularum, Sirmio, insularumque
ocelle, quascumque in liquentibus stagnis
marique uasto fert uterque Neptunus,
quam te libenter quamque laetus inuiso,
uix mi ipse credens Thuniam atque Bithynos
liquisse campos et uidere te in tuto.
o quid solutis est beatius curis,
cum mens onus reponit, ac peregrino
labore fessi uenimus larem ad nostrum,
desideratoque acquiescimus lecto?
hoc est quod unum est pro laboribus tantis.
salue, o uenusta Sirmio, atque ero gaude
gaudente, uosque, o Lydiae lacus undae,
ridete quidquid est domi cachinnorum.

XXXII

Amabo, mea dulcis Ipsitilla,
meae deliciae, mei lepores,
iube ad te ueniam meridiatum.
et si iusseris, illud adiuuato,
ne quis liminis obseret tabellam,
neu tibi lubeat foras abire,
sed domi maneas paresque nobis
nouem continuas fututiones.
uerum si quid ages, statim iubeto:
nam pransus iaceo et satur supinus
pertundo tunicamque palliumque.

31

Bright jewel of headlands, islands on the seas
And Neptune's lakes, oh Sirmio, you shine
Sparkling and beautiful, of restful ease
And joy. The thought that you are mine
Turns all my cares into untold delights
On seeing you again. Can it be true
I'm safe at last among familiar sights,
Bithynian plains have faded from my view?
How blessed to put cares away from mind
And rest again on my familiar bed,
To come back home from distant toil to find
That this is where my toil has always led.
So hail, dear Sirmio, delight with me,
Laugh with your master, hold your sides in glee.

32

Ipsithilla, baby girl,
Sugar, honey, let me curl
Up with you this afternoon,
Tell me that I can come soon,
Tell me none will bar your door,
That you're not busy, and what's more
That you will wait for me and choose
To give me nine successive screws.
Oh, don't delay, don't make me wait,
I'm resting, stuffed with all I ate,
Feeling my pecker stand up straight.

XXXIII

O furum optime balneariorum
Vibenni pater et cinaede fili
(nam dextra pater inquinatiore,
culo filius est uoraciore),
cur non exilium malasque in oras
itis? quandoquidem patris rapinae
notae sunt populo, et natis pilosas,
fili, non potes asse uenditare.

XXXIV

Dianae sumus in fide
puellae et pueri integri:
Dianam pueri integri
      puellaeque canamus.

o Latonia, maximi
magna progenies Iouis,
quam mater prope Deliam
      deposiuit oliuam,

montium domina ut fores
siluarumque uirentium
saltuumque reconditorum
      amniumque sonantum:

tu Lucina dolentibus
Iuno dicta puerperis,
tu potens Triuia et notho es
      dicta lumine Luna.

tu cursu, dea, menstruo
metiens iter annuum.
rustica agricolae bonis
      tecta frugibus exples.

33

Best thieves within the bathhouse door,
Vibennius and his fairy son:
The quicker dad's hand is, the more
His son's ass fucks for everyone.
Go look for some queer country where
You wretches aren't known so well;
Here all know dad's light-fingered flair,
So sonny's hairy ass won't sell.

34

In Diana's care,
Good girls and boys, we sing
Of Diana, pure and fair,
In our caroling.

Sweet daughter of great Jove,
In Delos by the sea,
Latona bore you, child of love,
Beside the olive tree

To be queen of the hills
And forests, which have stood
For centuries, of mountain rills,
Of hidden grove and wood.

Girls call, in birth's travail:
Lucina Juno, know
That Trivia brings help, and wail
For Luna's healing glow.

Great goddess, you divide
The year into its parts,

sis quocumque tibi placet
sancta nomine, Romulique,
antique ut solita es, bona
    sospites ope gentem.

XXXV

Poetae tenero, meo sodali,
uelim Caecilio, papyre, dicas
Veronam ueniat, Noui relinquens
Comi moenia Lariumque litus.
nam quasdam uolo cogitationes
amici accipiat sui meique.
quare, si sapiet, uiam uorabit,
quamuis candida milies puella
euntem reuocet, manusque collo
ambas iniciens roget morari.
quae nunc, si mihi uera nuntiantur,
illum deperit impotente amore.
nam quo tempore legit incohatam
Dindymi dominam, ex eo misellae
ignes interiorem edunt medullam.
ignosco tibi, Sapphica puella
musa doctior; est enim uenuste
Magna Caecilio incohata Mater.

You fill our storehouses, provide
Rich harvests with your arts.

Each name your greatness bears
We pray to, goddess: give
Your help to Romulus' heirs
So all, like him, may live.

35

Letter, tell Caecilius,
My poet friend, to come around,
Tell him that he, Verona bound,
Should leave the Novum Comum walls,
Tear up roads from Lake Larius;
We have a friend, if he recalls,
Whose words we ought to listen to,
Although our poet's girl has charms
And holds him tight with both her arms
And laughing, begs him to delay;
If what they say to me is true
She's now consumed with love. They say
That since she's read his poetry,
Unfinished though it is, a flame
Devours her soul. I cannot blame
You, Sapphic girl, more gifted than
The poet's muse; we all agree
His *Magna Mater*'s well—begun.

XXXVI

Annales Volusi, cacata carta,
uotum soluite pro mea puella.
nam sanctae Veneri Cupidinique
uouit, si sibi restitutus essem
desissemque truces uibrare iambos,
electissima pessimi poetae
scripta tardipedi deo daturam
infelicibus ustulanda lignis.
et hoc pessima se puella uidit
iocose lepide uouere diuis.
nunc o caeruleo creata ponto,
quae sanctum Idalium Vriosque apertos
quaeque Ancona Cnidumque harundinosam
colis quaeque Amathunta quaeque Golgos
quaeque Durrachium Hadriae tabernam,
acceptum face redditumque uotum,
si non illepidum neque inuenustum est.
at uos interea uenite in ignem,
pleni ruris et inficetiarum
annales Volusi, cacata carta.

XXXVII

Salax taberna uosque contubernales,
a pilleatis nona fratribus pila,
solis putatis esse mentulas uobis,
solis licere, quidquid est puellarum,
confutuere et putare ceteros hircos?
an, continenter quod sedetis insulsi
centum an ducenti, non putatis ausurum
me una ducentos irrumare sessores?
atqui putate: namque totius uobis

36

Volusius, your shitty sheets
Should pay a vow made by my girl,
Who swore, by Venus' son, to hurl
The best of the worst poet's feats
(If only I returned to her,
Stopped throwing savage javelins
Of iambs), yes, she'd toss my sins
In Vulcan's sullen forge to stir.
This bad girl knew her oath to be
Insulting to the gods and me.

    Oh goddess, born of ocean dark or light blue,
    Who inhabits blest Idalium,
    Storm beaten Urii and Ancona too
    And reed-bearing Cnidus,
    The cathouse of the Adriatic, Dyrrachium,
    Consider her oath fulfilled, and you can see
    I write my verses not unwittily.

Now then, clumsy poems, burn,
You wretched, rustic grunts and bleats,
Volusius, your shitty sheets.

37

You barflies of that crummy tavern, who
Raise so much hell, you're nine short posts from where
The brothers Castor, Pollux, get their due,
Do you think, fatheads, only you can bare
Your pricks and screw the girls, and all
The rest of us are only goats, because
Your silly clique, swelled up with nasty gall,
Hangs out together, a loud, stupid force
Of one or two hundred? You think I now

frontem tabernae sopionibus scribam.
puella nam mi, quae meo sinu fugit,
amata tantum quantum amabitur nulla,
pro qua mihi sunt magna bella pugnata,
consedit istic. hanc boni beatique
omnes amatis, et quidem, quod indignum est,
omnes pusilli et semitarii moechi;
tu praeter omnes une de capillatis,
cuniculosae Celtiberiae fili,
Egnati, opaca quem bonum facit barba
et dens Hibera defricatus urina.

XXXVIII

Malest, Cornifici, tuo Catullo,
malest, me hercule, et laboriose,
et magis magis in dies et horas.
quem tu, quod minimum facillimumque est,
qua solatus es allocutione?
irascor tibi. sic meos amores?
paulum quid lubet allocutionis,
maestius lacrimis Simonideis.

XXXIX

Egnatius, quod candidos habet dentes,
renidet usque quaque. si ad rei uentum est
subsellium, cum orator excitat fletum,
renidet ille; si ad pii rogum fili

Won't dare to fuck you all and fix the score?
Just sit there in a row! You'll also soon see how
I scrawl your peckers on the tavern door!
    My girl, who runs from my embrace, has left
    Me flat: who else would be insane as I,
    Who fought for her so hard—and am bereft?
    She hangs around your joint and is not shy,
    But sleeps with pimps who crawl the streets at night,
    And screws for all your gang, both low and high,
    Ignatius worst of all. It's his delight
    To brag of rabbity Spanish forebears; he
    Thinks that a bushy beard, teeth brushed with piss
    Make him a man of parts. Well, I agree,
    Of private parts, and what a prick is this!

38

Your poor old friend Catullus is not well,
Oh Cornificius, not well, not well:
By Hercules, each hour's a deeper hell,
And you, what comfort do you mean to be?
A kindly word is comfort. You can tell
I'm angry. Well, your love seems cool to me
Who need affection. Let your quick tears well,
Tears of Simonides, and make me well.

39

Ignatius, whose teeth are white
As snow, displays them well. Thus he
Will smile when lawyers rant, indict
Some wretch. He smiles if he should see

lugetur, orba cum flet unicum mater,
renidet ille. quidquid est, ubicumque est,
quodcumque agit, renidet: hunc habet morbum,
neque elegantem, ut arbitror, neque urbanum.
quare monendum est te mihi, bone Egnati.
si urbanus esses aut Sabinus aut Tiburs
aut pinguis Vmber aut obesus Etruscus
aut Lanuuinus ater atque dentatus
aut Transpadanus, ut meos quoque attingam,
aut quilubet, qui puriter lauit dentes,
tamen renidere usque quaque te nollem:
nam risu inepto res ineptior nulla est.
nunc Celtiber es: Celtiberia in terra,
quod quisque minxit, hoc sibi solet mane
dentem atque russam defricare gingiuam,
ut, quo iste uester expolitior dens est,
hoc te amplius bibisse praedicet loti.

XL

Quaenam te mala mens, miselle Rauide,
agit praecipitem in meos iambos?
quis deus tibi non bene aduocatus
uecordem parat excitare rixam?
an ut peruenias in ora uulgi?
quid uis? qualubet esse notus optas?
eris, quandoquidem meos amores
cum longa uoluisti amare poena.

A mother mourn her only son.
He smiles and smiles no matter when
Or where. This custom is not one
Of elegant or urbane men.
Ignatius, I caution you,
Were you Sabine, Tiburtian,
Or Umbrian, or that fat crew
Of Tuscans, or of my own clan
Beside the Po, if you're of folk
Like these who clean their teeth quite well,
I still would think your grin no joke,
For smiles so out of place all smell.
Now you're a Spaniard, and in Spain
You piss and brush your teeth with it,
Your gums as well, and so again,
You brush with piss, which suits a smiling shit.

40

What, Ravidus, you stupid ass,
Has thrown you up against my verse;
What hostile god has brought you, worse
Than quarrelsome, out of your class?
Do you intend to win renown,
To be the gossip's favorite?
You'll earn much grief since your poor wit
Told you to steal my love, you clown.

XLI

Ameana puella defututa
tota milia me decem poposcit,
ista turpiculo puella naso,
decoctoris amica Formiani.
propinqui, quibus est puella curae,
amicos medicosque conuocate:
non est sana puella, nec rogare
qualis sit solet aes imaginosum.

XLII

Adeste, hendecasyllabi, quot estis
omnes undique, quotquot estis omnes.
iocum me putat esse moecha turpis,
et negat mihi nostra reddituram
pugillaria, si pati potestis.
persequamur eam et reflagitemus.
quae sit, quaeritis? illa, quam uidetis
turpe incedere, mimice ac moleste
ridentem catuli ore Gallicani.
circumsistite eam, et reflagitate,
"moecha putida, redde codicillos,
redde, putida moecha, codicillos!"
non assis facis? o lutum, lupanar,
aut si perditius potes quid esse.
sed non est tamen hoc satis putandum.
quod si non aliud potest, ruborem
ferreo canis exprimamus ore.
conclamate iterum altiore uoce
"moecha putida, redde codicillos,
redde, putida moecha, codicillos!"
sed nil proficimus, nihil mouetur.

41

Ameana, big nosed twat
Duns me for an awful lot,
Mamurra's mistress, that damn shit
Wants my bankroll, every bit.
Find out what the hell has shocked her,
Call her relatives, her doctor,
Give that slut a looking glass
To show her face looks like her ass.

42

All of you syllables, come on,
Quick, form a line in close array,
To march against a slut whose fun
Is snitching poems from me. Flay
Her, teach the nasty slob that she
Must give my tablets back to me.
Who is she then? Why, she's the crumb
Who struts around the crowded street
And shakes her ass; her grin is dumb,
She gapes, a Gallic bitch in heat.
Surround her, tell her plainly she
Had better give my verse to me.
What, no? That filthy, fucked-out whore!
She doesn't give a damn for that?
Well, I will fix her ten times more,
And ten times louder, "Spiteful cat,
You whore, give back my poetry,
You cunt, return my verse to me!"
It's still no good! She doesn't care:
I'll have to try another way,
Abuse won't work although I spare

mutanda est ratio modusque uobis,
siquid proficere amplius potestis:
"pudica et proba, redde codicillos."

XLIII

Salve, nec minimo puella naso
nec bello pede nec nigris ocellis
nec longis digitis nec ore sicco
nec sane nimis elegante lingua,
decoctoris amica Formiani.
ten prouincia narrat esse bellam?
tecum Lesbia nostra comparatur?
o saeclum insapiens et infacetum!

XLIV

O funde noster seu Sabine seu Tiburs
(nam te esse Tiburtem autumant, quibus non est
cordi Catullum laedere; at quibus cordi est,
quouis Sabinum pignore esse contendunt),
sed seu Sabine siue uerius Tiburs,
fui libenter in tua suburbana
uilla, malamque pectore expuli tussim,
non inmerenti quam mihi meus uenter,
dum sumptuosas appeto, dedit, cenas.
nam, Sestianus dum uolo esse conuiua,
orationem in Antium petitorem
plenam ueneni et pestilentiae legi.
hic me grauedo frigida et frequens tussis
quassauit usque, dum in tuum sinum fugi,
et me recuraui otioque et urtica.

No effort. Well, I'll have to say,
"Oh, sweet, pure virgin, hear my plea,
Oh, please return my poetry!"

43

Hello, you girl whose nose grew well,
With big, fat feet and beady eyes,
Squat fingers, sloppy mouth whose smell
Can overcast the clearest skies,
Hard-up Mamurra's listless screw,
Are you a doll by Gallic rules,
Is Lesbia compared to you?
Oh, what an age of tasteless fools!

44

Oh, dear old farm, Sabine or Tiburtine
(My friends say Tiburtine, but there are those
Who love annoying me, and say Sabine),
But Tiburtine, Sabine, I'm glad I chose
You for a rest between the countryside
And city, where I soon got well again,
Shook off this cough that I could not abide,
Which I, through my sheer greed, contracted when
I went to gorge at Sestius' house
And read his tirade on a candidate,
One Antius. He called the guy a louse,
And scanning through his poisoned flow of hate
I caught a wretched chill and racking cough;
So here I came and in your bosom found
The strength to shake that double sickness off

quare refectus maximas tibi grates
ago, meum quod non es ulta peccatum.
nec deprecor iam, si nefaria scripta
Sesti recepso, quin grauedinem et tussim
non mi, sed ipsi Sestio ferat frigus,
qui tunc uocat me, cum malum librum legi.

XLV

Acmen Septimius suos amores
tenens in gremio "mea" inquit "Acme,
ni te perdite amo atque amare porro
omnes sum assidue paratus annos,
quantum qui pote plurimum perire,
solus in Libya Indiaque tosta
caesio ueniam obuius leoni."
hoc ut dixit, Amor sinistra ut ante
dextra sternuit approbationem.

at Acme leuiter caput reflectens
et dulcis pueri ebrios ocellos
illo purpureo ore suauiata,
"sic," inquit "mea uita Septimille,
huic uni domino usque seruiamus,
ut multo mihi maior acriorque
ignis mollibus ardet in medullis."
hoc ut dixit, Amor sinistra ut ante
dextra sternuit approbationem.

nunc ab auspicio bono profecti
mutuis animis amant amantur.
unam Septimius misellus Acmen
mauult quam Syrias Britanniasque:
uno in Septimio fidelis Acme

By dieting on nettle broth, grew sound
And lazy. Now, you dear old house, I'm fine,
And I must thank you for your kindly aid;
But if I read another lousy line
By Sestius, may he at once be paid,
Not I, with coughing spasms and with pain,
For I won't read his junk before we dine again.

45

Septimius held Acme tight
Against his heart, said, "Oh, my love,
I swear by all the gods above,
If I don't wish I always might
Forever love you and be yours,
Then all alone, I pray I meet
A green-eyed lion in the heat
Of far-off India's sun scorched shores,
Or else, in Libya may I die."
Upon this, Love, from left to right,
Approving, sneezed, as well he might.
Then Acme kissed her darling guy
On his moist eyes. With ruby lips
She spoke: "My life, Septimius,
Let's always serve the love god thus;
Oh, how this sweetest passion drips
Into my heart." When she said this,
Love, as before, from left to right,
Sneezed once again, as well he might.
By these good auspices, their bliss
Was smoothed, and Acme is his love,
Not Syria, Britain, which confer
Great wealth on each adventurer,

facit delicias libidinesque.
quis ullos homines beatiores
uidit, quis Venerem auspicatiorem?

XLVI

Iam uer egelidos refert tepores,
iam caeli furor aequinoctialis
iucundis Zephyri silescit auris.
linquantur Phrygii, Catulle, campi
Nicaeaeque ager uber aestuosae:
ad claras Asiae uolemus urbes.
iam mens praetrepidans auet uagari,
iam laeti studio pedes uigescunt.
o dulces comitum ualete coetus,
longe quos simul a domo profectos
diuersae uarie uiae reportant.

XLVII

Porci et Socration, duae sinistrae
Pisonis, scabies famesque mundi,
uos Veraniolo meo et Fabullo
uerpus praeposuit Priapus ille?
uos conuiuia lauta sumptuose
de die facitis, mei sodales
quaerunt in triuio uocationes?

And Acme swears by all above
That she for poor Septimius yearns;
Each lover to the other turns:
How blessed is their love, how bright their passion burns.

46

The chill of spring grows mild again,
The frenzied, wintry winds are gone;
Warm zephyrs gently urge me on:
"Catullus go, leave Phrygian
Encampments, rich Nicean lands
Far, far behind." Then let us fly
Through Asian cities, we who sigh
To wander and to leave these strands;
How my feet dance with restlessness!
Farewell, oh sweet companions all,
Each answering a different call,
And hastening home with eagerness.

47

Socration and Porcius, oh you
Choice goons of Piso, rascals through and through,
You glutted leeches, has that hard on shown
You favor, not Fabullus nor my own
Veranius? Does pricko give you two
Money for gaudy, daylong feasts while, all unknown,
My friends must freeload as the beggars do?

XLVIII

Mellitos oculos tuos, Iuuenti,
si quis me sinat usque basiare,
usque ad milia basiem trecenta
nec numquam uidear satur futurus,
non si densior aridis aristis
sit nostrae seges osculationis.

XLIX

Disertissime Romuli nepotum,
quot sunt quotque fuere, Marce Tulli,
quotque post aliis erunt in annis,
gratias tibi maximas Catullus
agit pessimus omnium poeta,
tanto pessimus omnium poeta,
quanto tu optimus omnium patronus.

L

Hesterno, Licini, die otiosi
multum lusimus in meis tabellis,
ut conuenerat esse delicatos:
scribens uersiculos uterque nostrum
ludebat numero modo hoc modo illoc,
reddens mutua per iocum atque uinum.
atque illinc abii tuo lepore
incensus, Licini, facetiisque,
ut nec me miserum cibus iuuaret
nec somnus tegeret quiete ocellos,
sed toto indomitus furore lecto
uersarer, cupiens uidere lucem,

48

Juventius, if I could kiss your eyes
A million times, I'd seek those honeyed flowers
Again and yet again, and pass my hours
Returning for more nectar. I'd devise
More kisses than the richest harvest yields
In grain from ripest ears in autumn fields.

49

Marcus Tullius, most skilled in speech
Of all the heirs of Romulus, of each
Who is, who has been, or will ever be,
Catullus offers you warm thanks, if he,
The worst of poets may; best advocate,
I'm worst by just as much as you're most great.

50

Licinius, at leisure yesterday
Amid our tablets, in poetic play,
Fastidious companions, we amused
Ourselves with verses which we took and used
In varying meters, now this way, now that,
And jokes and wine kept them from growing flat.
My friend, inflamed by both your wit and charm,
I left when you'd inflicted so much harm
On me, that I lost all my appetite
And couldn't sleep a wink throughout the night;
But I kept tossing all about my bed
And longed for dawn to raise her drowsy head,

ut tecum loquerer simulque ut essem.
at defessa labore membra postquam
semimortua lectulo iacebant,
hoc, iucunde, tibi poema feci,
ex quo perspiceres meum dolorem.
nunc audax caue sis, precesque nostras,
oramus, caue despuas, ocelle,
ne poenas Nemesis reposcat a te.
est uehemens dea: laedere hanc caueto.

LI

Ille mi par esse deo uidetur,
ille, si fas est, superare diuos,
qui sedens aduersus identidem te
    spectat et audit

dulce ridentem, misero quod omnis
eripit sensus mihi: nam simul te,
Lesbia, aspexi, nihil est super mi
    vocis in ore

lingua sed torpet, tenuis sub artus
flamma demanat, sonitu suopte
tintinant aures, gemina teguntur
    lumina nocte.

otium, Catulle, tibi molestum est:
otio exsultas nimiumque gestis:
otium et reges prius et beatas
    perdidit urbes.

That I might once more find myself with you,
But after such travail the whole night through
I lay stretched out, half living and half dead:
Too sick to come, I send this verse instead.
Dear friend, on reading this you'll plainly see
How strong my anguish is. Be kind to me,
Old fellow. Don't despise my little gift.
Now stop! Before you offer me short shrift,
Bear Nemesis in mind for she is stern,
And for my love give love back in return.

51

He seems the equal of the gods,
To my poor judgment, even more,
Who sits beside you, hears your sweet voice pour
    Out laughter, and he nods,

Approves, while my heart aches and I,
I've lost my sense on seeing you,
Oh Lesbia, I find I'm tongue-tied too,
    And look on, mute and shy.

I cannot speak, a flame's caress
Spreads slowly through my limbs, shrill sounds
Ring in my ears, a double night confounds
    My eyes in dizziness.

Catullus, you are all excess,
You surge with hopes, sink in despairs;
The fall of ancient realms and royal heirs
    Came through such wantonness.

LII

Quid est, Catulle? quid moraris emori?
sella in curuli struma Nonius sedet,
per consulatum peierat Vatinius:
quid est, Catulle? quid moraris emori?

LIII

Risi nescio quem modo e corona,
qui, cum mirifice Vatiniana
meus crimina Caluos explicasset,
admirans ait haec manusque tollens,
"di magni, salaputium disertum!"

LIV

Othonis caput oppido est pusillum,

 * * * * *

et eri rustice semilauta crura,
subtile et leue peditum Libonis,

 * * * * *

si non omnia, displicere uellem
tibi et Fuficio seni recocto . . .

 * * * * *

irascere iterum meis iambis
inmerentibus, unice imperator.

52

Catullus, now's the time to croak;
Is Nonius in office now,
Vatinius consul? What a joke!
Catullus, now's the time to croak.

53

Just now I laughed at someone who
Was listening as dear Calvus drew
A portrait, deadly through and through
Of that Vatinius; his hands flew
Up: "What a gabby midget—whew!"

54

Otho's head is strangely small.

* * * * *

His master's shitty, rustic legs,
And Libo's farts will choke us all.

* * * * *

Old slob Fuficius, you're not so hot;
Nor you. I'll needle both if they do not.

* * * * *

Caesar, iambics seem to anger you;
Should they, unique commander? But they do.

LV

Oramus, si forte non molestum est,
demonstres ubi sint tuae tenebrae.
te Campo quaesiuimus minore,
te in Circo, te in omnibus libellis,
te in templo summi Iouis sacrato.
in Magni simul ambulatione
femellas omnes, amice, prendi,
quas uultu uidi tamen sereno.
a vel te, sic ipse flagitabam,
Camerium mihi pessimae puellae.
quaedam inquit, nudum reduc . . .
"en hic in roseis latet papillis."
sed te iam ferre Herculei labos est;
tanto te in fastu negas, amice.
dic nobis ubi sis futurus, ede
audacter, committe, crede luci.
nunc te lacteolae tenent puellae?
si linguam clauso tenes in ore,
fructus proicies amoris omnes.
uerbosa gaudet Venus loquella.
uel, si uis, licet obseres palatum,
dum uestri sim particeps amoris.

55

If I may ask without offense,
Where's your hangout? I've had looks
In marketplaces, at the dense
And crowded race track, and where books
Are bought and sold, and when I'd go
To Jove's great temple: where were you?
I searched in Pompey's portico
And asked the chicks, more than a few,
Where I could find you, but no go,
When I said, "Where's Camerius,
You wicked broads," one answered, "Oh,
I've got him here where he won't fuss,
Between my rosy nipples." Well,
To seek and find you would deplete
The strength of Hercules. Oh, hell,
I simply don't know where we'd meet;
So tell me where you're hiding out,
And say it freely, don't be shy.
Can't milk white girls all do without
You? Are you really all that sly?
If you're so quiet, then you may
Lose out, for Venus loves the guy
Who's got a line; but you're okay
If mutual love's the reason why.

LVI

O rem ridiculam, Cato, et iocosam,
dignamque auribus et tuo cachinno!
ride quidquid amas, Cato, Catullum:
res est ridicula et nimis iocosa.
deprendi modo pupulum puellae
trusantem; hunc ego, si placet Dionae,
protelo rigida mea cecidi.

LVII

Pulcre conuenit improbis cinaedis,
Mamurrae pathicoque Caesarique.
nec mirum: maculae pares utrisque,
urbana altera et illa Formiana,
impressae resident nec eluentur:
morbosi pariter, gemelli utrique,
uno in lecticulo erudituli ambo,
non hic quam ille magis uorax adulter,
riuales socii puellularum.
pulcre conuenit improbis cinaedis.

LVIII

Caeli, Lesbia nostra, Lesbia illa,
illa Lesbia, quam Catullus unam
plus quam se atque suos amauit omnes,
nunc in quadriuiis et angiportis
glubit magnanimi Remi nepotes.

56

Oh Cato, here's a funny thing
To make you laugh until you're sick,
And have you howl just like a hick,
It's more absurd than anything:
I caught this young shit in the grass
Screwing his girl, and ran my prick,
Just like a spear, right up his ass.

57

These lecherous fags are of one kind,
Mamurra and his Caesar; they
Are both great splotches; there's no way
To cleanse them. One's at Rome; you'll find
The other twin at Formiae:
But there's one bed in which both lie.
These pedants are in rivalry,
But share the cute young cunt they find;
They're better matched than such as we,
These lecherous fags are of one kind.

58

Caelius, our Lesbia, this Lesbia, yes
That Lesbia, whom your Catullus won
And loved more than himself in his excess.
Dark alleys see her shamelessness,
Where now she gladly fucks with everyone.

LVIIIA

Non custos si fingar ille Cretum,
non Ladas ego pinnipesue Perseus,
non si Pegaseo ferar uolatu,
non Rhesi niueae citaeque bigae;
adde huc plumipedas uolatilesque,
uentorumque simul require cursum,
quos iunctos, Cameri, mihi dicares:
defessus tamen omnibus medullis
et multis languoribus peresus
essem te mihi, amice, quaeritando.

LIX

Bononiensis Rufa Rufulum fellat,
uxor Meneni, saepe quam in sepulcretis
uidistis ipso rapere de rogo cenam,
cum deuolutum ex igne prosequens panem
ab semiraso tunderetur ustore.

LX

Num te leaena montibus Libystinis
aut Scylla latrans infima inguinum parte
tam mente dura procreauit ac taetra,
ut supplicis uocem in nouissimo casu
contemptam haberes, a nimis fero corde?

58A

If I were guardian of Crete,
Like Pegasus, were borne in flight,
Like Ladas, Perseus, were fleet,
Like Rhesus steeds, were swift and light,
If you, Camerius, could send
Me winged feet that I might fly,
Could bind the lawless winds to lend
Me, yet bone tired, I would sigh,
Exhausted and worn out, my friend,
In that damned search for you which has no end.

59

Bolognese Rufa sucks her Rufus; has a spouse
Menenius. She haunts the local graveyards where
She robs the funeral pyres of food. This goddam louse
Will chase the loaves of bread that roll down from the flames:
The sloppy slave in charge gives her her lumps: he knows
        those games.

60

From what Libyan mountain lion were you born;
From what Scylla with its horrid, howling womb
That you're so hard of heart? Why, you would scorn
A suppliant, though you should see the tomb
Gape wide for him, oh blackest soul yet born.

LXI

Collis o Heliconii
cultor, Vraniae genus,
qui rapis teneram ad uirum
uirginem, o Hymenaee Hymen,
    o Hymen Hymenaee;

cinge tempora floribus
suaue olentis amaraci,
flammeum cape laetus, huc
huc ueni, niueo gerens
    luteum pede soccum;

excitusque hilari die,
nuptialia concinens
uoce carmina tinnula,
pelle humum pedibus, manu
    pineam quate taedam.

namque Vinia Manlio,
qualis Idalium colens
uenit ad Phrygium Venus
iudicem, bona cum bona
    nubet alite uirgo,

floridis uelut enitens
myrtus Asia ramulis
quos Hamadryades deae
ludicrum sibi roscido
    nutriunt umore.

quare age, huc aditum ferens,
perge linquere Thespiae
rupis Aonios specus,
nympha quos super irrigat
    frigerans Aganippe.

61

Great god of Helicon,
Urania's son,
You snatch a young girl to be wed
And lay her in a husband's bed,
    Oh Hymen, god of marriage.

Head crowned with marjoram,
Take veil and come,
And wear the saffron slippers too
Upon your snow white feet, for you
    Are Hymen, god of marriage.

Arise upon this day
For joyous play
And dancing, raise your voice and sing
Sweet nuptial melodies, and bring
    And shake the torch of marriage.

So Vinia comes now
And makes her vow,
Lovely as Venus when she came
Before her Trojan judge; proclaim
    Good omens at her marriage.

Like Asian myrtle, bright
In golden light,
Which hamadryads, as they play,
Nourish with dew throughout the day,
    So she is at her marriage.

Prepare yourself to go
From Aganippe's flow
Whose waters through Thespian boulders wind;
Now leave Aeonian caves behind;
    Do not delay your marriage.

ac domum dominam uoca
coniugis cupidam noui,
mentem amore reuinciens,
ut tenax hedera huc et huc
    arborem implicat errans.

uosque item simul, integrae
uirgines, quibus aduenit
par dies, agite in modum
dicite, o Hymenaee Hymen,
    o Hymen Hymenaee.

ut lubentius, audiens
se citarier ad suum
munus, huc aditum ferat
dux bonae Veneris, boni
    coniugator amoris.

quis deus magis anxiis
est petendus amantibus?
quem colent homines magis
caelitum, o Hymenaee Hymen,
    o Hymen Hymenaee?

te suis tremulus parens
inuocat, tibi uirgines
zonula soluunt sinus,
te timens cupida nouus
    captat aure maritus.

tu fero iuueni in manus
floridam ipse puellulam
dedis a gremio suae
matris, o Hymenaee Hymen,
    o Hymen Hymenaee.

Call home the bride to be
And let her see
Her love, and bind her heart; evoke
The ivy's love that clings to oak,
    So be it with this marriage.

Unmarried virgins, you
Sing with me too;
For each of you a day like this
Will come, and so, to mark their bliss,
    Sing, "Hymen, god of marriage."

Thus he, the herald of
The goddess, Love,
Shall come to us more eagerly
And join these honest lovers: we
    Now call the god of marriage.

What god do we adore,
Who is sought more
Than all the other gods on high
By mortal lovers, as they sigh
    For Hymen, god of marriage.

Old fathers, in their dread
Of sons unwed
Invoke you; girls in shy delight
Loosen their girdles, and, in fright,
    The groom awaits his marriage.

You snatch the fresh young bride
From her mom's side,
And give her beauty, youth, and grace
To her wild husband's hot embrace,
    Oh Hymen, god of marriage.

nil potest sine te Venus,
fama quod bona comprobet,
commodi capere, at potest
te uolente. quis huic deo
    compararier ausit?

nulla quit sine te domus
liberos dare, nec parens
stirpe nitier; at potest
te uolente. quis huic deo
    compararier ausit?

quae tuis careat sacris,
non queat dare praesides
terra finibus: at queat
te uolente. quis huic deo
    compararier ausit?

claustra pandite ianuae.
uirgo adest. uide ut faces
splendidas quatiunt comas?

.   .   .   .

.   .   .   .

.   .   .   .

.   .   .   .

tardet ingenuus pudor:
quem tamen magis audiens,
    flet quod ire necesse est.

flere desine. non tibi Au-
runculeia periculum est,
ne qua femina pulcrior
clarum ab Oceano diem
    uiderit uenientem.

Without you, Venus gives
No joy that lives
In honest love, but loves to nod
On unions you approve. What god
 Dares match himself with you?

Without your grace, no one
Can have a son,
But if, approvingly, you nod,
No home is childless then. What god
 Dares match himself with you?

A land without your care
Comes to despair:
None guard her borders, but is strong
When you are present, and as long;
 Who'll match himself with you?

Now throw the portal wide,
Here comes the bride,
And see the torches dance and shake
Their fiery tresses for her sake,
 Oh Hymen, god of marriage.

Does she still hesitate
To join her mate?
Does she, in shyness, still delay,
And listening weeps that she today
 Must come now to her marriage?

Aurunculeia, hear:
Put all your fear
Aside and let the bridegroom see
The loveliest of brides, and be
 The happier for marriage.

talis in uario solet
diuitis domini hortulo
stare flos hyacinthinus.
sed moraris, abit dies.
     prodeas noua nupta.

prodeas noua nupta, si
iam uidetur, et audias
nostra uerba. uide ut faces
aureas quatiunt comas:
     prodeas noua nupta.

non tuus leuis in mala
deditus uir adultera,
probra turpia persequens,
a tuis teneris uolet
     secubare papillis,

lenta sed uelut adsitas
uitis implicat arbores,
implicabitur in tuum
complexum. sed abit dies:
     prodeas noua nupta.

o cubile, quod omnibus

.   .   .   .

.   .   .   .

.   .   .   .

     candido pede lecti,

quae tuo ueniunt ero,
quanta gaudia, quae uaga
nocte, quae medio die
gaudeat! sed abit dies:
     prodeas noua nupta.

As hyacinth takes root
With sturdy shoot
Within its garden, you stand fast,
Delaying, though the day is past:
    Come forth, new bride, for marriage.

Come forth, come forth, new bride,
And do not hide,
But hear us, see the torches shake
Their golden tresses for your sake,
    Come forth, new bride, for marriage.

Your husband will not leave
Your arms nor grieve
You with a paramour, nor burn
With other passions, but will turn
    To your soft breasts in marriage.

But as the vine clasped tree
So shall he be
Closely embraced by both your arms,
But see, it's late, bring forth your charms,
    Come out, oh bride, for marriage.

Oh bridal bed, you call
In turn to all,
But most to her who now will put
The slipper from her snow white foot
    And seek the bed of marriage.

What joy he'll have, what fun,
Now day is done
And soft night shadows fall, and then
When daylight comes around again;
    Come forth, new bride, for marriage.

tollite, o pueri, faces:
flammeum uideo uenire.
ite concinite in modum
"io Hymen Hymenaee io,
    io Hymen Hymenaee."

ne diu taceat procax
Fescennina iocatio,
nec nuces pueris neget
desertum domini audiens
    concubinus amorem.

da nuces pueris, iners
concubine! satis diu
lusisti nucibus: lubet
iam seruire Talasio.
    concubine, nuccs da.

sordebant tibi uilicae,
concubine, hodie atque heri:
nunc tuum cinerarius
tondet os. miser a miser
    concubine, nuces da.

diceris male te a tuis
unguentate glabris marite
abstinere, sed abstine.
io Hymen Hymenaee io,
    io Hymen Hymenaee.

scimus haec tibi quae licent
sola cognita, sed marito
ista non eadem licent.
io Hymen Hymenaee io,
    io Hymen Hymenaee.

Raise up the torches, boys,
And sing their joys,
I see, I see the bridal veil,
Raise up the torches then, and hail
    Our Hymen, god of marriage.

Let bawdy Fescennine
Jokes be a sign
His favored boy shall give out nuts
To all, for Manlius now shuts
    Himself away in marriage.

So, favored boy, today
Give nuts away,
You can't have nuts to play with, thus
You now must serve Talassius
    And bow to him in marriage.

Yet not so long ago
You wouldn't go
With country girls, but now your face
Needs shaving; so, poor wretch, give place
    To Hymen, god of marriage.

Bridegroom, your slaves declare
That you won't care
To give them up as lovers now;
But you'll abstain and keep your vow
    To Hymen, god of marriage.

We know what you have done
Was only fun,
But, truly, you are married now,
And those are fields you must not plow,
    Oh Hymen, god of marriage.

nupta, tu quoque quae tuus
uir petet caue ne neges,
ni petitum aliunde eat.
io Hymen Hymenaee io,
    io Hymen Hymenaee.

en tibi domus ut potens
et beata uiri tui,
quae tibi sine seruiat
(io Hymen Hymenaee io,
    io Hymen Hymenaee)

usque dum tremulum mouens
cana tempus anilitas
omnia omnibus annuit.
io Hymen Hymenaee io,
    io Hymen Hymenaee.

transfer omine cum bono
limen aureolos pedes,
rasilemque subi forem.
io Hymen Hymenaee io,
    io Hymen Hymenaee.

aspice intus ut accubans
uir tuus Tyrio in toro
totus immineat tibi.
io Hymen Hymenaee io,
    io Hymen Hymenaee.

illi non minus ac tibi
pectore uritur intimo
flamma, sed penite magis.
io Hymen Hymenaee io,
    io Hymen Hymenaee.

You also, bride, must do
What's sought of you,
Or he may seek another bed,
And find his pleasure there, instead
    Of finding it in marriage.

See how rich and great
Is the estate
He offers you. Then be content,
And here, as mistress, give consent
    To Hymen, god of marriage.

'Til old age, crowned with snow,
Shaking and slow,
Forces your trembling head to nod
Assent to all; then to the god
    Sing Hymen, lord of marriage.

Your golden-slippered feet,
So light and fleet,
Will bring good omens as you come
Within the polished door, your home,
    Sing Hymen, god of marriage.

The groom waits eagerly
For you, and see,
He's on a purple couch, and there
He thinks of you alone, I swear
    By Hymen, god of marriage.

Within him glows the fire
That mounts up higher
Than that within your secret heart
Where passion burns; now seek the art
    Of Hymen, god of marriage.

mitte brachiolum teres,
praetextate, puellulae:
iam cubile adeat uiri.
io Hymen Hymenaee io,
    io Hymen Hymenaee.

uos bonae senibus uiris
cognitae bene feminae
collocate puellulam.
io Hymen Hymenaee io,
    io Hymen Hymenaee.

iam licet uenias, marite:
uxor in thalamo tibi est,
ore floridulo nitens,
alba parthenice uelut
    luteumuc papauer.

at, marite, ita me iuuent
caelites, nihilo minus
pulcer es, neque te Venus
neglegit. sed abit dies:
    perge, ne remorare.

non diu remoratus es:
iam uenis. bona te Venus
iuuerit, quoniam palam
quod cupis cupis, et bonum
    non abscondis amorem.

ille pulueris Africi
siderumque micantium
subducat numerum prius,
qui uestri numerare uolt
    multa milia ludi.

So, boy, release her arm,
For all her charm
Is ready for his bed alone
For he'll be hers, she'll be his own
    And Hymen's, god of marriage.

Now set her in her place
For his embrace,
You matrons who've been married long
And married well, with ties made strong
    By Hymen, god of marriage.

Your wife is in her home:
Now, bridegroom, come,
She waits for you within the bed
A golden poppy, newlywed,
    A lily at her marriage.

But so are you, by heaven,
As fair as even
She is. Lovely Venus deigned
To give you grace. But day has waned,
    Go, consummate your marriage.

You don't delay for long
But quick and strong
You come. May Venus help you now,
For you have both been joined; your vow
    Will bind your hearts in marriage.

And he who counts your joys,
He best employs
His count on grains of sand in far-
Off Africa, or counts each star
    Which shines upon your marriage.

ludite ut lubet, et breui
liberos date. non decet
tam uetus sine liberis
nomen esse, sed indidem
    semper ingenerari.

Torquatus uolo paruulus
matris e gremio suae
porrigens teneras manus
dulce rideat ad patrem
    semihiante labello.

sit suo similis patri
Manlio et facile insciis
noscitetur ab omnibus,
et pudicitiam suae
    matris indicet ore.

talis illius a bona
matre laus genus approbet,
qualis unica ab optima
matre Telemacho manet
    fama Penelopeo.

claudite ostia, uirgines:
lusimus satis. at boni
coniuges, bene uiuite et
munere assiduo ualentem
    exercete iuuentam.

LXII

Vesper adest, iuuenes, consurgite: Vesper Olympo
exspectata diu uix tandem lumina tollit.
surgere iam tempus, iam pinguis linquere mensas,

Indulge your happiness,
And soon caress
Your children, for your passion's flame
Preserves your ancient line and name;
    Be fruitful in your marriage.

Upon his mommy's knee
I'd love to see
Torquatus stretch small hands to dad
And smile and laugh, a merry lad,
    The flower of this marriage.

And Manlius, just see
Your image: he
Is recognized by everyone,
The child of honor and your son,
    The issue of your marriage.

Through his mother, may he know
Much fame, for so
Telemachus was justly praised,
Whom chaste Penelope had raised,
    An honor to her marriage.

It's time to shut the door
And laugh no more,
We've laughed enough; now, happy pair,
Live and love, and loving bear
    The children of your marriage.

62

The evening star is shining; young men, rise:
It now beams down its long awaited light
Upon our solemn joy; young men, arise,

iam ueniet uirgo, iam dicetur hymenaeus.
Hymen o Hymenaee, Hymen ades o Hymenaee!

Cernitis, innuptae, iuuenes? consurgite contra;
nimirum Oetaeos ostendit Noctifer ignes.
sic certest; uiden ut perniciter exsiluere?
non temere exsiluere, canent quod uincere par est.
Hymen o Hymenaee, Hymen ades o Hymenaee!

Non facilis nobis, aequales, palma parata est;
aspicite, innuptae secum ut meditata requirunt.
non frustra meditantur: habent memorabile quod sit;
nec mirum, penitus quae tota mente laborant.
nos alio mentes, alio diuisimus aures;
iure igitur uincemur: amat uictoria curam.
quare nunc animos saltem conuertite uestros;
dicere iam incipient, iam respondere decebit.
Hymen o Hymenaee, Hymen ades o Hymenaee!

Hespere, quis caelo fertur crudelior ignis?
qui natam possis complexu auellere matris,
complexu matris retinentem auellere natam,
et iuueni ardenti castam donare puellam.
quid faciunt hostes capta crudelius urbe?
Hymen o Hymenaee, Hymen ades o Hymenaee!

Hespere, quis caelo lucet iucundior ignis?
qui desponsa tua firmes conubia flamma,
quae pepigere uiri, pepigerunt ante parentes,
nec iunxere prius quam se tuus extulit ardor.
quid datur a diuis felici optatius hora?
Hymen o Hymenaee, Hymen ades o Hymenaee!

Hesperus e nobis, aequales, abstulit unam.

     *   *   *   *   *

namque tuo aduentu uigilat custodia semper,

Arise from rich repasts and turn your sight
Upon the bride who comes; let us recite
And sing the sacred marriage hymn before her eyes.

Young women, do you see the men? Arise
And meet them, for the holy evening star
Now blazes. Do you see them lightly rise?
How confident their bearing is; all are
Worthy of these rites, which none will mar
Who sing the sacred marriage hymn before your eyes.

Companions listen: how their voices rise
In practiced song; we shall not easily
Be victors, for their soaring notes arise
In virgin singing, true and pure and free
And sweet with fruits of study; we may see
Ourselves defeated if we are not wise
And do not sing in our most solemn key,
And rightly will they crown their enterprise
If we do not do well in our replies,
When they sing the sacred marriage hymn before our eyes.

Oh evening star, what other fire can rise
And be so cruel, sundering the clasp
Of daughters and their mothers, can devise
Such grief, can send a chaste young girl to gasp
In passion's arms, as in a tyrant's grasp?
She now hears the sacred marriage hymn with tear-dimmed
        eyes.

Oh evening star, arise in joy, arise;
Your fire makes firm the sacred marriage rite,
Now husbands' vows confirm the parents'; rise
As all await your advent and your light;
For heaven offers us no sweeter sight
To sanctify the sacred marriage hymn before our eyes.

nocte latent fures, quos idem saepe reuertens,
Hespere, mutato comprendis nomine Eous.
at lubet innuptis ficto te carpere questu.
quid tum, si carpunt, tacita quem mente requirunt?
Hymen o Hymenaee, Hymen ades o Hymenaee!

Vt flos in saeptis secretus nascitur hortis,
ignotus pecori, nullo conuolsus aratro,
quem mulcent aurae, firmat sol, educat imber;
multi illum pueri, multae optauere puellae:
idem cum tenui carptus defloruit ungui,
nulli illum pueri, nullae optauere puellae:
sic uirgo, dum intacta manet, dum cara suis est;
cum castum amisit polluto corpore florem,
nec pueris iucunda manet, nec cara puellis.
Hymen o Hymenaee, Hymen ades o Hymenaee!

Vt uidua in nudo uitis quae nascitur aruo,
numquam se extollit, numquam mitem educat uuam,
sed tenerum prono deflectens pondere corpus
iam iam contingit summum radice flagellum;
hanc nulli agricolae, nulli coluere iuuenci:
at si forte eadem est ulmo coniuncta marito,
multi illam agricolae, multi coluere iuuenci:
sic uirgo dum intacta manet, dum inculta senescit;
cum par conubium maturo tempore adepta est,
cara uiro magis et minus est inuisa parenti.
Hymen o Hymenaee, Hymen ades o Hymenaee!

Et tu ne pugna cum tali coniuge, uirgo.
non aequom est pugnare, pater cui tradidit ipse,
ipse pater cum matre, quibus parere necesse est.
uirginitas non tota tua est, ex parte parentum est,
tertia pars patri, pars est data tertia matri,

Oh evening star, that shines in these dark skies,
You've stolen one of us . . .

  * * * * *

Oh evening star, your signal lights these skies
And tells the guard to watch throughout the night
For thieves; you often take them by surprise,
Coming upon them in the pale dawn's light
As morning star. So, too, love's thieves delight
In their embraces, sought before your eyes.
The maiden's voice complains about this sight
Which you allow, but we know otherwise:
They love to do what they say they despise.
Now let them sing the sacred marriage hymn before our eyes.

The flowering bud, within the hedge, may rise,
To bloom untouched by grazing herd or plough,
But soothed by winds, the golden sun, the skies,
With falling rain, this bud the youths all vow
To pluck, but once torn from its garden, how
It withers! Boys and girls all turn their eyes
Away, but gladly will approve her who is now
An untouched virgin, fully grown and wise,
For none would wish to wed her otherwise.
Let us sing the sacred marriage hymn before her eyes.

In barren fields, no vine can ever rise,
No blossom forms, no ripeness fills the fruit,
But turning its slim form in arching wise,
Its topmost stem bends down to touch its root,
And none will cultivate its downcast shoot.
But if the elm and vine will solemnize
Their union, then all honor them, salute
Their flowering joy. Thus virgins, marriage ties
Will bind you to a man whom you should prize,
So let us sing the sacred marriage hymn before all eyes.

tertia sola tua est: noli pugnare duobus,
qui genero sua iura simul cum dote dederunt.
Hymen o Hymenaee, Hymen ades o Hymenaee!

LXIII

Super alta uectus Attis celeri rate maria,
Phrygium ut nemus citato cupide pede tetigit
adiitque opaca siluis redimita loca deae,
stimulatus ibi furenti rabie, uagus animis,
deuoluit ili acuto sibi pondera silice,
itaque ut relicta sensit sibi membra sine uiro,
etiam recente terrae sola sanguine maculans,
niueis citata cepit manibus leue typanum,
typanum tuum, Cybebe, tua, mater, initia,
quatiensque terga tauri teneris caua digitis
canere haec suis adorta est tremebunda comitibus.
"agite ite ad alta, Gallae, Cybeles nemora simul,
simul ite, Dindymenae dominae uaga pecora,
aliena quae petentes uelut exules loca
sectam meam exsecutae duce me mihi comites
rapidum salum tulistis truculentaque pelagi,
et corpus euirastis Veneris nimio odio;
hilarate erae citatis erroribus animum.
mora tarda mente cedat: simul ite, sequimini
Phrygiam ad domum Cybebes, Phrygia ad nemora deae,
ubi cymbalum sonat uox, ubi tympana reboant,
tibicen ubi canit Phryx curuo graue calamo,

Oh maiden, teach yourself to harmonize
With him your father chose to join you to,
And even as you're lovely, then be wise:
Oh virgin, just as you are pure, be true;
Virginity is born in triple guise,
Is shared alike by parents and by you.
Your gentlest ways are now your husband's due,
So join us: sing the sacred marriage hymn before our eyes.

63

Upon the fleet ship, Attis rapidly flew
Eager to find the sacred Phrygian grove,
And in its deepest shade, great Cybele drew
Him madly onward till he, shuddering, drove
A flint into his groin, and staggering back
He wailed for his lost manhood, shrieked in a fire
Of pain. The stain of hot blood reddened the black,
Cold earth, and her white hands in maddened desire
Then seized the sacred tambour, Cybele's horn
And trumpet, struck the hollow, echoing hide
With slender hands; to her companions, reborn,
She sang, "Now come, who would with Cybele bide
In lofty groves together. Dindymus' herd,
You chattels of our mistress, wandered and found
Your exile at an end, at Cybele's word;
You sailed on raging seas when you were all bound
For refuge to these groves. My followers all,
You, loathing bonds of love, castrated yourselves
To gladden your goddess' heart, so now, at her call,
Cast all doubt from your minds. Let us quicken ourselves
As we approach the home of the Phrygian queen,
While tambour loudly sounds and praises arise,

ubi capita Maenades ui iaciunt hederigerae,
ubi sacra sancta acutis ululatibus agitant,
ubi sueuit illa diuae uolitare uaga cohors,
quo nos decet citatis celerare tripudiis."
    simul haec comitibus Attis cecinit notha mulier,
thiasus repente linguis trepidantibus ululat,
leue tympanum remugit, caua cymbala recrepant,
uiridem citus adit Idam properante pede chorus.
furibunda simul anhelans uaga uadit animam agens
comitata tympano Attis per opaca nemora dux,
ueluti iuuenca uitans onus indomita iugi;
rapidae ducem sequuntur Gallae properipedem.
itaque, ut domum Cybebes tetigere lassulae,
nimio e labore somnum capiunt sine Cerere.
piger his labante languore oculos sopor operit;
abit in quiete molli rabidus furor animi.
sed ubi oris aurei Sol radiantibus oculis
lustrauit aethera album, sola dura, mare ferum,
pepulitque noctis umbras uegetis sonipedibus,
ibi Somnus excitam Attin fugiens citus abiit;
trepidante eum recepit dea Pasithea sinu.
ita de quiete molli rapida sine rabie
simul ipsa pectore Attis sua facta recoluit,
liquidaque mente uidit sine quis ubique foret,
animo aestuante rusum reditum ad uada tetulit.
ibi maria uasta uisens lacrimantibus oculis,
patriam allocuta maestast ita uoce miseriter.
    "patria o mei creatrix, patria o mea genetrix,
ego quam miser relinquens, dominos ut erifugae
famuli solent, ad Idae tetuli nemora pedem,
ut aput niuem et ferarum gelida stabula forem,
et earum omnia adirem furibunda latibula,
ubinam aut quibus locis te positam, patria, reor?
cupit ipsa pupula ad te sibi derigere aciem,

As carved flutes sadly sing in the echoing green;
Here maenads, ivy crowned, and uttering cries,
Toss heads in holy rites, distracted and gaunt,
And wander these dim slopes with quick, flying feet;
Now let us all stream in a flood to the votaries' haunt."
    The counterfeit woman thus chanted: all trembled to meet
The goddess, then in fright they suddenly wailed
With palsied tongues; the tambour loudly resounded,
And they ran, shouting, to Ida as bright daylight paled,
As Attis led them all. Her mind was confounded
By frenzied madness; panting and gasping, she fled;
The tambour called, she heard, a young heifer who
Abhors the yoke, is filled with unspeakable dread.
The Gallae, fleet of foot, all following, flew
With Attis to the crest, great Cybele's home,
Where they sank wearily. Exhaustion's deep sleep
Fell fast upon their eyes before they could roam
To find their food. Now silent, they lay deep
In slumber; soothed and lulled, their souls were free.
But when the bright-faced sun, all glowing and red,
Rose, shone on air, hard earth, tumultuous sea,
As he climbed up, the shades of blackest night fled
From Phaëthon's horses: Somnus left Attis to day,
And was received against Pasithea's heart.
Now Attis rose from rest, her rage at a stay,
And sadly, in her mind, considered her part,
And clearly saw her deeds and where she was now;
Her mind distraught, she went to the shore once again,
Through tears, she saw vast seas, regretted her vow,
And in her anguished soul, remembering when
Her manhood was intact, she then spoke at last:
    "Oh land in which I lived, oh mother of mine,
Alas that I left you behind, for here I'm held fast;
A runaway slave, I formed a futile design,

rabie fera carens dum breue tempus animus est.
egone a mea remota haec ferar in nemora domo?
patria, bonis, amicis, genitoribus abero?
abero foro, palaestra, stadio et gymnasiis?
miser a miser, querendum est etiam atque etiam, anime.
quod enim genus figuraest, ego non quod obierim?
ego mulier, ego adolescens, ego ephebus, ego puer,
ego gymnasi fui flos, ego eram decus olei:
mihi ianuae frequentes, mihi limina tepida,
mihi floridis corollis redimita domus erat,
linquendum ubi esset orto mihi Sole cubiculum.
ego nunc deum ministra et Cybeles famula ferar?
ego Maenas, ego mei pars, ego uir sterilis ero?
ego uiridis algida Idae niue amicta loca colam?
ego uitam agam sub altis Phrygiae columinibus,
ubi cerua siluicultrix, ubi aper nemoriuagus?
iam iam dolet quod egi, iam iamque paenitet."
　　roseis ut huic labellis sonitus citus abiit,
geminas deorum ad aures noua nuntia referens,
ibi iuncta iuga resoluens Cybele leonibus
laeuumque pecoris hostem stimulans ita loquitur.
"agedum," inquit "age ferox i, fac ut hunc furor agitet,
fac uti furoris ictu reditum in nemora ferat,
mea libere nimis qui fugere imperia cupit.
age caede terga cauda, tua uerbera patere,
fac cuncta mugienti fremitu loca retonent,
rutilam ferox torosa ceruice quate iubam."
ait haec minax Cybebe religatque iuga manu.
ferus ipse sese adhortans rapidum incitat animo,
uadit, fremit, refringit uirgulta pede uago.
at ubi umida albicantis loca litoris adiit,
teneramque uidit Attin prope marmora pelagi,
facit impetum. illa demens fugit in nemora fera;
ibi semper omne uitae spatium famula fuit.

And sought Mount Ida's snows, wild beasts in their lairs,
For I, in madness, strove to confront them all.
My eye looks to my homeland, but it despairs
Of seeing athletic fields and the games I recall,
While my mind briefly now is lucid and clear.
Must I be always here, so far from my land,
My parents, friends, possessions, all I hold dear?
How wretched is my lot on this far-off strand!
What human form is there which I have not had?
A woman, man, youth, boy, I've been every one,
Who once was manly and an athlete too, clad
In victor's garb. The wrestling matches I've won!
I well recall how once my doors were sought out,
My house festooned with many garlands of flowers;
Once I arose with morning, and went about
At leisure, who now am a victim of Cybele's powers,
A handmaid to the gods, as Cybele wills.
Can I be part of myself, a eunuch, a slave,
A maenad? Must I live upon snowy hills,
Seek out on Ida's slopes some Phrygian cave,
And dwell close by its peaks with the shy woodland doe,
In forests where great boars run wild in the glade?
I deeply regret what I've done and my heart's filled with woe."
    She sadly spoke, and ceased her hopeless tirade,
But her words rose from earth to Cybele's ear;
The goddess turned to where her yoked lions stood
And freed both of the beasts that all cattle fear;
With these harsh words she bade that one of them should
Go: "Now quickly, fierce one, see that he's driven away
In madness to the grove. Does he long to be free?
Go quickly, angry one, spread fear and dismay,
Let forests reecho your roaring, let all creatures flee,
As, ruffling your mane, you make your frightful advance."
When she said this, the beast leapt free of his yoke,

dea, magna dea, Cybebe, dea domina Dindymi,
procul a mea tuos sit furor omnis, era, domo:
alios age incitatos, alios age rabidos.

LXIV

Peliaco quondam prognatae uertice pinus
dicuntur liquidas Neptuni nasse per undas
Phasidos ad fluctus et fines Aeeteos,
cum lecti iuuenes, Argiuae robora pubis,
auratam optantes Colchis auertere pellem
ausi sunt uada salsa cita decurrere puppi,
caerula uerrentes abiegnis aequora palmis.
diua quibus retinens in summis urbibus arces
ipsa leui fecit uolitantem flamine currum,
pinea coniungens inflexae texta carinae.
illa rudem cursu prima imbuit Amphitriten;
quae simul ac rostro uentosum proscidit aequor
tortaque remigio spumis incanuit unda,
emersere freti candenti e gurgite uultus
aequoreae monstrum Nereides admirantes.
illa, siqua alia, uiderunt luce marinas
mortales oculis nudato corpore Nymphas
nutricum tenus exstantes e gurgite cano.
tum Thetidis Peleus incensus fertur amore,
tum Thetis humanos non despexit hymenaeos,

His spirit kindled by her furious glance,
And raging, he ran and roared, and whirling he broke
His stride off short, until he reached the wet sand
And charged straight at Attis, brooding by the seaside,
Who ran off madly to the forested land,
And was a slave until the day that he died.

Oh goddess of great Dindymus, oh Cybele,
Drive others to such frenzy, make others roam,
But let my heart be free, stay far off from my home.

64

On Pelion's summit grew the stalwart trees
Which long ago, they say, first swam the seas,
And skimmed on Neptune's crystal tides to bring
Themselves to Phasis, where there was a king,
Aeëtes, who possessed the Golden Fleece,
Desired by Argive youth, the flower of Greece,
Who dared to sail the briny sea, dared stir
Its azure blue expanse with oars of fir.
Athena who protects the citadel,
Designed the keel of pine and bowed it well,
Created that first craft to plow the ocean's swell.
The ship then plunged her prow through windy seas;
Her oars churned through the white-flecked foam with ease,
And Nereids raised up their heads to see
And wonder at this latest prodigy.
And then, if ever, mortals had a sight
Of mermaids, bobbing in the sun's bright light,
Their rosy nipples just above the swell.
So Peleus saw Thetis and he fell
In love with her; and she desired to wed

tum Thetidi pater ipse iugandum Pelea sensit.
o nimis optato saeclorum tempore nati
heroes, saluete, deum genus! o bona matrum
progenies, saluete iterum . . .
uos ego saepe, meo uos carmine compellabo.
teque adeo eximie taedis felicibus aucte,
Thessaliae columen Peleu, cui Iuppiter ipse,
ipse suos diuum genitor concessit amores;
tene Thetis tenuit pulcerrima Nereine?
tene suam Tethys concessit ducere neptem,
Oceanusque, mari totum qui amplectitur orbem?

     quae simul optatae finito tempore luces
aduenere, domum conuentu tota frequentat
Thessalia, oppletur laetanti regia coetu:
dona ferunt prae se, declarant gaudia uultu.
deseritur Cieros, linquunt Phthiotica Tempe
Crannonisque domos ac moenia Larisaea,
Pharsalum coeunt, Pharsalia tecta frequentant.
rura colit nemo, mollescunt colla iuuencis,
non humilis curuis purgatur uinea rastris,
non glebam prono conuellit uomere taurus,
non falx attenuat frondatorum arboris umbram,
squalida desertis rubigo infertur aratris.
ipsius at sedes, quacumque opulenta recessit
regia, fulgenti splendent auro atque argento.
candet ebur soliis, collucent pocula mensae,
tota domus gaudet regali splendida gaza.
puluinar uero diuae geniale locatur
sedibus in mediis, Indo quod dente politum
tincta tegit roseo conchyli purpura fuco.

     haec uestis priscis hominum uariata figuris
heroum mira uirtutes indicat arte.
namque fluentisono prospectans litore Diae,
Thesea cedentem celeri cum classe tuetur

This mortal man without the slightest dread,
For Zeus was pleased that she went to another's bed.
Oh heroes born in better times, all hail!
You are the noble subjects of my tale;
Oh sons of gods and mortal mothers too,
I'll often pause, address myself to you,
To you, brave Peleus, most of all, because
The father of the gods himself once was
In love with Thetis who becomes your wife,
With Jove's own blessing for a happy life.
So Nereus' lovely daughter is content
To be your bride, as Tethys nods assent
And so does Ocean who surrounds the land.
The happy wedding day is now at hand,
And in the palace, all of Thessaly
Is welcome, voices echo merrily:
The guests bear gifts and show they are delighted,
Phthiotic Tempe, Cieros, stand deserted.
Now Crannon's homes and old Larissa's walls
Are left by folk who throng Pharsalian halls.
The land's untilled, the bullock's soft and slow,
The vineyards choke for no one wields the hoe,
The field's no longer scarred by ox or plough
And pruning hooks neglect the leafy bough,
While ploughshares lying idle soon corrode.
But see the contrast in the king's abode
Resplendent with the glow of wealth untold
In ivory thrones and gleaming cups of gold.
The palace proudly shows its treasures since
The marriage couch of Thetis and her prince
Awaits within. Its graceful ivory frame
Is spread with richest coverlets. The flame
Of crimson dyes them; they're embroidered, tell
A tale of heroes, artfully and well.

indomitos in corde gerens Ariadna furores,
necdum etiam sese quae uisit uisere credit,
utpote fallaci quae tum primum excita somno
desertam in sola miseram se cernat harena.
immemor at iuuenis fugiens pellit uada remis,
irrita uentosae linquens promissa procellae.
quem procul ex alga maestis Minois ocellis,
saxea ut effigies bacchantis, prospicit, eheu,
prospicit et magnis curarum fluctuat undis,
non flauo retinens subtilem uertice mitram,
non contecta leui uelatum pectus amictu,
non tereti strophio lactentis uincta papillas,
omnia quae toto delapsa e corpore passim
ipsius ante pedes fluctus salis alludebant.
sed neque tum mitrae neque tum fluitantis amictus
illa uicem curans toto ex pectore, Theseu,
toto animo, tota pendebat perdita mente.
a misera, assiduis quam luctibus externauit
spinosas Erycina serens in pectore curas,
illa tempestate, ferox quo ex tempore Theseus
egressus curuis e litoribus Piraei
attigit iniusti regis Gortynia templa.
    nam perhibent olim crudeli peste coactam
Androgeoneae poenas exsoluere caedis
electos iuuenes simul et decus innuptarum
Cecropiam solitam esse dapem dare Minotauro.
quis angusta malis cum moenia uexarentur,
ipse suum Theseus pro caris corpus Athenis
proicere optauit potius quam talia Cretam
funera Cecropiae nec funera portarentur.
atque ita naue leui nitens ac lenibus auris
magnanimum ad Minoa uenit sedesque superbas.
hunc simul ac cupido conspexit lumine uirgo
regia, quam suauis exspirans castus odores

Here Ariadne gazes frantically
On Dia's shore, she scans the angry sea,
Sees Theseus departing with his fleet,
While frenzy racks her heart with every beat.
She can't believe her eyes which just before
Dispelled deluding sleep. Upon the shore
She sees herself abandoned and alone
While he now plies his oars; his heart's a stone
And he has cast his vows to every wind,
While statue-like, aware how he has sinned,
She stands upon the beach, can only stare,
Her bosom agonized by woe and care;
Her coif no longer hides the flaxen tress
And look—her milk white breasts are bared—her dress
And girdle, fallen to her feet now ride
As idle playthings on the surging tide.
She's heedless, Theseus, of everything,
Her mind and heart are numbed by Venus' sting
And dwell on you alone. Her love's in vain
And serves to pierce her breast with thorns of pain.
What grief she's known since Theseus first sailed
From Athens' harbor, came to Crete and hailed
The unjust king whose violence prevailed.
        It's told how long ago a pestilence
Compelled all Athens to make recompense
For murdering Androgeos. They sent
The Minotaur a yearly complement
Of youths and maidens as a sacrifice.
But Athens could not bear so great a price,
So Theseus sets out himself, contrives
To spare his city those most precious lives.
The swiftest ship and fairest winds soon bring
Him to the halls of Minos, Crete's proud king.
As soon as she sees him, the princess falls

lectulus in molli complexu matris alebat,
quales Eurotae praecingunt flumina myrtus
auraue distinctos educit uerna colores,
non prius ex illo flagrantia declinauit
lumina, quam cuncto concepit corpore flammam
funditus atque imis exarsit tota medullis.
heu misere exagitans immiti corde furores
sancte puer, curis hominum qui gaudia misces,
quaeque regis Golgos quaeque Idalium frondosum,
qualibus incensam iactastis mente puellam
fluctibus, in flauo saepe hospite suspirantem!
quantos illa tulit languenti corde timores!
quanto saepe magis fulgore expalluit auri,
cum saeuum cupiens contra contendere monstrum
aut mortem appeteret Theseus aut praemia laudis!
non ingrata tamen frustra munuscula diuis
promittens tacito succepit uota labello.
nam uelut in summo quatientem brachia Tauro
quercum aut conigeram sudanti cortice pinum
indomitus turbo contorquens flamine robur,
eruit (illa procul radicitus exturbata
prona cadit, late quaeuis cumque obuia frangens),
sic domito saeuum prostrauit corpore Theseus
nequiquam uanis iactantem cornua uentis.
inde pedem sospes multa cum laude reflexit
errabunda regens tenui uestigia filo,
ne labyrintheis e flexibus egredientem
tecti frustraretur inobseruabilis error.

     sed quid ego a primo digressus carmine plura
commemorem, ut linquens genitoris filia uultum,
ut consanguineae complexum, ut denique matris,
quae misera in gnata deperdita laetabatur,
omnibus his Thesei dulcem praeoptarit amorem:
aut ut uecta rati spumosa ad litora Diae

In love. Brought up within these palace walls,
A lovely creature, the queen's pampered hope,
As fragrant as the myrtle on the slope
Along Eurotas' flood, as filled with scents
As sweet as those the breath of spring presents,
No sooner had she turned away her gaze
From him, than Venus' all-consuming blaze
Flared up within her heart: it's Cupid's ploy
To plague poor humans with cares mixed with joy.
At Golgi and Idalium are fanes
Of Venus who has caused this girl such pains
That she so often sighed for her fair guest.
How many fears she felt within her breast!
Her face became more pale than gold when she
Saw him go forth to meet his enemy,
The Minotaur, and seek his victory.
In silence she made prayers to gods above
Which rose like incense from the fire of love.
The gods looked after him, neglected her.
But as on Taurus' heights the winds bestir
Themselves and topple resin bearing pine
Or sturdy oak, which, crashing, falls supine
And crushes all before it, far and wide,
So Theseus then felled the Bull, which tried
To gore him, tossing horns to no avail.
Then bravest Theseus by that thin trail
Of thread, retraced his steps within the maze,
The labyrinth, and solved its winding ways.
        But why have I strayed from my theme? Should I
Relate just how a daughter chose to fly
Far from her father's face, her sister's love,
Her mother, so distressed at the loss of
Her daughter, who preferred the love instead
Of Theseus? Shall I tell how they fled

uenerit, aut ut eam deuinctam lumina somno
liquerit immemori discedens pectore coniunx?
saepe illam perhibent ardenti corde furentem
clarisonas imo fudisse e pectore uoces,
ac tum praeruptos tristem conscendere montes,
unde aciem in pelagi uastos protenderet aestus,
tum tremuli salis aduersas procurrere in undas
mollia nudatae tollentem tegmina surae,
atque haec extremis maestam dixisse querellis,
frigidulos udo singultus ore cientem;
"sicine me patriis auectam, perfide, ab aris,
perfide, deserto liquisti in litore, Theseu?
sicine discedens neglecto numine diuum,
immemor a! deuota domum periuria portas?
nullane res potuit crudelis flectere mentis
consilium? tibi nulla fuit clementia praesto,
immite ut nostri uellet miserescere pectus?
at non haec quondam blanda promissa dedisti
uoce mihi, non haec miserae sperare iubebas,
sed conubia laeta, sed optatos hymenaeos,
quae cuncta aerii discerpunt irrita uenti.
nunc iam nulla uiro iuranti femina credat,
nulla uiri speret sermones esse fideles;
quis dum aliquid cupiens animus praegestit apisci,
nil metuunt iurare, nihil promittere parcunt:
sed simul ac cupidae mentis satiata libido est,
dicta nihil metuere, nihil periuria curant.
certe ego te in medio uersantem turbine leti
eripui, et potius germanum amittere creui,
quam tibi fallaci supremo in tempore dessem.
pro quo dilaceranda feris dabor alitibusque
praeda, neque iniacta tumulabor mortua terra.
quaenam te genuit sola sub rupe leaena,
quod mare conceptum spumantibus exspuit undis,

To Dia's foam-flecked shores, how while she slept
Her lover left her, proved himself adept
At treachery? Her poor heart was inflamed;
They say she often shrieked at him and blamed
Him for her state; she would ascend some peak
Or rugged crag, and soon she'd sadly seek
To cast her gaze upon the waters, then
She'd scramble to the water's edge again
And lifting skirts above her naked knee,
With sighs and sobs she would cry plaintively:
"So you've deserted me upon this shore,
False, faithless wretch, forgetting what you swore
To god? You carry home your perjury?
What might have turned your mind from cruelty?
Was there no mercy in your soul to move
Your cruel heart to pity? How you prove
That all your softly spoken words were lies:
You bade me hope for happy marriage ties;
Such words are tatters in a wintry gust
And what men swear no woman now may trust.
How men will swear to anything if they
Conceive desire; but once they've had their way,
And once their pressing lust is satisfied,
They're heedless of the fact that they have lied.
I snatched you from the jaws of death; what's more:
For you I let my brother die; you bore
Me off, abandoned me to be the prey
Of birds and beasts when death will come my way.
My corpse will know no sepulcher, no earth
Will cover it. What lioness gave birth
To you within her den? What seas conceived
And spewed you forth? What Syrtis, Scylla heaved
And moaned when whelping such a one as you?
For saving you, you've deemed that death's my due?

quae Syrtis, quae Scylla rapax, quae uasta Carybdis,
talia qui reddis pro dulci praemia uita?
si tibi non cordi fuerant conubia nostra,
saeua quod horrebas prisci praecepta parentis,
attamen in uestras potuisti ducere sedes,
quae tibi iucundo famularer serua labore,
candida permulcens liquidis uestigia lymphis,
purpureaue tuum consternens ueste cubile.
sed quid ego ignaris nequiquam conquerar auris,
externata malo, quae nullis sensibus auctae
nec missas audire queunt nec reddere uoces?
ille autem prope iam mediis uersatur in undis,
nec quisquam apparet uacua mortalis in alga.
sic nimis insultans extremo tempore saeua
fors etiam nostris inuidit questibus auris.
Iuppiter omnipotens, utinam ne tempore primo
Gnosia Cecropiae tetigissent litora puppes,
indomito nec dira ferens stipendia tauro
perfidus in Cretam religasset nauita funem,
nec malus hic celans dulci crudelia forma
consilia in nostris requiesset sedibus hospes!
nam quo me referam? quali spe perdita nitor?
Idaeosne petam montes? at gurgite lato
discernens ponti truculentum diuidit aequor.
an patris auxilium sperem? quemne ipsa reliqui
respersum iuuenem fraterna caede secuta?
coniugis an fido consoler memet amore?
quine fugit lentos incuruans gurgite remos?
praeterea nullo colitur sola insula tecto,
nec patet egressus pelagi cingentibus undis.
nulla fugae ratio, nulla spes: omnia muta,
omnia sunt deserta, ostentant omnia letum.
non tamen ante mihi languescent lumina morte,
nec prius a fesso secedent corpore sensus,

If wedded life with me repels you so
Because your father still keeps you in tow,
At least you might have brought me home to be
Your loving slave in all humility.
It would have brought me so much joy to soothe
Your tired feet with coolest waters, smooth
The crimson coverlet upon your bed.
Now why should I though overwhelmed by dread
Entrust my cries to winds that can't perceive
Or answer me? He's long since taken leave
Of me and sailed across the sea's expanse.
And now no human shape will ever chance
To come and comfort me in any way
For death will be my lot this very day.
O Jupiter, would that the Attic fleet
Had never landed on the shores of Crete,
With its grim tribute to the fearsome Bull.
For then the captain with his heart so full
Of lies would not have been our guest! His face
Was comely, no one dreamed that he'd disgrace
Us all. Where can I go? Is there no hope
For me? Can I seek out some mountain slope
In Crete? The savage seas keep me away.
Could I hope for my father's help one day?
I left his house with that adventurer,
My lover, my dear brother's murderer.
Console myself with his fidelity?
With straining oars, he's fled away from me!
There is no shelter on this barren shore,
No way at all to leave this place, what's more
There is no hope, no signs of life, no sounds
But all is doomed; the mark of death abounds.
Yet death will never dim my eyes nor will
My senses slip away from me until

quam iustam a diuis exposcam prodita multam
caelestumque fidem postrema comprecer hora.
quare facta uirum multantes uindice poena
Eumenides, quibus anguino redimita capillo
frons exspirantis praeportat pectoris iras,
huc huc aduentate, meas audite querellas,
quas ego, uae misera, extremis proferre medullis
cogor inops, ardens, amenti caeca furore.
quae quoniam uerae nascuntur pectore ab imo,
uos nolite pati nostrum uanescere luctum,
sed quali solam Theseus me mente reliquit,
tali mente, deae, funestet seque suosque."

    has postquam maesto profudit pectore uoces,
supplicium saeuis exposcens anxia factis,
annuit inuicto caelestum numine rector;
quo motu tellus atque horrida contremuerunt
aequora concussitque micantia sidera mundus.
ipse autem caeca mentem caligine Theseus
consitus oblito dimisit pectore cuncta,
quae mandata prius constanti mente tenebat,
dulcia nec maesto sustollens signa parenti
sospitem Erectheum se ostendit uisere portum.
namque ferunt olim, classi cum moenia diuae
linquentem gnatum uentis concrederet Aegeus,
talia complexum iuueni mandata dedisse:
"gnate mihi longa iucundior unice uita,
gnate, ego quem in dubios cogor dimittere casus,
reddite in extrema nuper mihi fine senectae,
quandoquidem fortuna mea ac tua feruida uirtus
eripit inuito mihi te, cui languida nondum
lumina sunt gnati cara saturata figura,
non ego te gaudens laetanti pectore mittam,
nec te ferre sinam fortunae signa secundae,
sed primum multas expromam mente querellas,

The gods have promised me most solemnly
That justice will be done, avenging me.
Come, Furies, come, and hear my just complaint;
Take vengeance now, away with all restraint!
The hissing snakes upon your brows reveal
The indignation which your hearts conceal.
Now hear the thoughts which well up in my mind,
So pitiful, so feverish and blind.
And since my heart now seeks surcease of pain
Do not allow my grief to flow in vain,
But just as Theseus deserted me
May he destroy himself unwittingly."

    In her great sorrow she had sought redress,
Due punishment, for all his wickedness.
So heaven's ruler nodded and approved
And by that nod the land and seas were moved,
The twinkling stars all trembled in the sky.
But Theseus' mind was enveloped by
The mists of dull oblivion which drained
His nimble wits of all they had retained,
So he forgot to give the sign that he
Had sighted Athens' harbor from the sea.
It's said that when Aegeus said farewell
To his dear son at Athens' citadel,
Instructed him, while clinging to his side:
"My only son, more dear than life, the pride
Of my extreme old age, now we must part;
I grieve that you must heed your eager heart,
Courageously departing from my sight
Before my eyes have taken full delight
In my strong son. So I, in my distress,
Shan't let you hoist the white sails of success.
But I must void my heart of sadness now
By sprinkling dust upon my furrowed brow,

canitiem terra atque infuso puluere foedans,
inde infecta uago suspendam lintea malo,
nostros ut luctus nostraeque incendia mentis
carbasus obscurata dicet ferrugine Hibera.
quod tibi si sancti concesserit incola Itoni,
quae nostrum genus ac sedes defendere Erecthei
annuit, ut tauri respergas sanguine dextram,
tum uero facito ut memori tibi condita corde
haec uigeant mandata, nec ulla oblitteret aetas;
ut simul ac nostros inuisent lumina collis,
funestam antennae deponant undique uestem,
candidaque intorti sustollant uela rudentes,
quam primum cernens ut laeta gaudia mente
agnoscam, cum te reducem aetas prospera sistet."
haec mandata prius constanti mente tenentem
Thesea ceu pulsae uentorum flamine nubes
aerium niuei montis liquere cacumen.
at pater, ut summa prospectum ex arce petebat,
anxia in assiduos absumens lumina fletus,
cum primum infecti conspexit lintea ueli,
praecipitem sese scopulorum e uertice iecit,
amissum credens immiti Thesea fato.
sic funesta domus ingressus tecta paterna
morte ferox Theseus, qualem Minoidi luctum
obtulerat mente immemori, talem ipse recepit.
quae tum prospectans cedentem maesta carinam
multiplices animo uoluebat saucia curas.

     at parte ex alia florens uolitabat Iacchus
cum thiaso Satyrorum et Nysigenis Silenis,
te quaerens, Ariadna, tuoque incensus amore.

.   .   .   .

quae tum alacres passim lymphata mente furebant
euhoe bacchantes, euhoe capita inflectentes.
harum pars tecta quatiebant cuspide thyrsos,

And draping your ship's mast with purple hue
In token of my burning grief for you.
The holy goddess, guardian of our race,
Inhabiting Itonus, by her grace
Decreed that you will slay the Bull of Crete.
So when its blood has drenched your hands and feet
Be sure to bear in mind your father's plea
Which you should brand upon your memory:
The moment that you spy these hills, then cast
Aside these purple sails from every mast
And hoist the white ones, signaling to me
The greatest day that I will ever see."
So Theseus at first remembered all
But soon his mind forgot, as in a squall
The clouds are blown from snowbound mountainsides.
His father on the city's heights now bides
His time and through his tears he finally
Perceives the sails that boded death, so he
Hurls himself headlong from the highest rock,
Believing Theseus had died. The shock
Of overwhelming grief to that degree
That Ariadne felt was now to be
The lot of Theseus forevermore.
For as his fleet retreated from her eyes,
She'd sealed his fate with shrill and anguished cries.

    The coverlet displayed another scene
In which the comely Bacchus, young and lean
With satyrs and Sileni, wandering
And seeking Ariadne for their king,
Was much in love with her.

    *   *   *   *   *

                                   All ran astray,
Tossing their heads and shouting: "Evoe!"
Some brandished bacchic wands with vine-sheathed points

pars e diuolso iactabant membra iuuenco,
pars sese tortis serpentibus incingebant,
pars obscura cauis celebrabant orgia cistis,
orgia quae frustra cupiunt audire profani;
plangebant aliae proceris tympana palmis,
aut tereti tenuis tinnitus aere ciebant;
multis raucisonos efflabant cornua bombos
barbaraque horribili stridebat tibia cantu.
    talibus amplifice uestis decorata figuris
puluinar complexa suo uelabat amictu.
quae postquam cupide spectando Thessala pubes
expleta est, sanctis coepit decedere diuis.
hic, qualis flatu placidum mare matutino
horrificans Zephyrus procliuas incitat undas,
Aurora exoriente uagi sub limina Solis,
quae tarde primum clementi flamine pulsae
procedunt leuiterque sonant plangore cachinni,
post uento crescente magis magis increbescunt,
purpureaque procul nantes ab luce refulgent:
sic tum uestibuli linquentes regia tecta
ad se quisque uago passim pede discedebant.
quorum post abitum princeps e uertice Pelei
aduenit Chiron portans siluestria dona:
nam quoscumque ferunt campi, quos Thessala magnis
montibus ora creat, quos propter fluminis undas
aura parit flores tepidi fecunda Fauoni,
hos indistinctis plexos tulit ipse corollis,
quo permulsa domus iucundo risit odore.
confestim Penios adest, uiridantia Tempe,
Tempe, quae siluae cingunt super impendentes,
Naiasin, linquens doris celebranda choreis,
non uacuos: namque ille tulit radicitus altas
fagos ac recto proceras stipite laurus,
non sine nutanti platano lentaque sorore

Some girt themselves with snakes or tossed the joints
Of mangled bullocks; some most solemnly
Concealed the sacred objects not to be
Revealed. Some beat their tambourines. A few
Made brazen cymbals clash while others blew
Into the deeply droning horns as shrill
Barbarian reeds screeched out their maddening trill.
    The coverlet with its embroidery
Adorned the marriage couch most splendidly.
So all the eager youth of Thessaly
Admired it and then gave way to be
Replaced by gods. Just as the west winds play
And ruffle seas before the break of day,
As waves build up Aurora seeks the door
Through which the lordly, rising sun will soar.
The ripples slowly rise; the gentle breeze
First nudges them to laughter, then its ease
Is turned to blasts which cleave the mounting swell
And form the far-flung waves which crash pell mell,
Reflecting purple hues from day's new light.
Just so the hall is left by every guest
Who sets out for his home to seek his rest.
And when they'd left the king of centaurs came
With woodland presents; Chiron was his name.
His presents were the flowers of the field
And those which Thessaly's high mountains yield
With river blossoms nurtured by the breeze.
He'd made them into wreaths that they might please
The royal household with their fragrant smell.
Peneus then arrived from Tempe's dell,
A place with overhanging ferns and trees
Where Naiads dance to Doric strains with ease.
Uprooted trees were gifts he brought with him,
Some lofty beeches, bay trees straight and slim,

flammati Phaethontis et aeria cupressu.
haec circum sedes late contexta locauit,
uestibulum ut molli uelatum fronde uireret.
post hunc consequitur sollerti corde Prometheus,
extenuata gerens ueteris uestigia poenae,
quam quondam silici restrictus membra catena
persoluit pendens e uerticibus praeruptis.
inde pater diuum sancta cum coniuge natisque
aduenit caelo, te solum, Phoebe, relinquens
unigenamque simul cultricem montibus Idri:
Pelea nam tecum pariter soror aspernata est,
nec Thetidis taedas uoluit celebrare iugalis.

    qui postquam niueis flexerunt sedibus artus,
large multiplici constructae sunt dape mensae,
cum interea infirmo quatientes corpora motu
ueridicos Parcae coeperunt edere cantus.
his corpus tremulum complectens undique uestis
candida purpurea talos incinxerat ora,
at roseae niueo residebant uertice uittae,
aeternumque manus carpebant rite laborem.
laeua colum molli lana retinebat amictum,
dextera tum leuiter deducens fila supinis
formabat digitis, tum prono in pollice torquens
libratum tereti uersabat turbine fusum,
atque ita decerpens aequabat semper opus dens,
laneaque aridulis haerebant morsa labellis,
quae prius in leui fuerant exstantia filo:
ante pedes autem candentis mollia lanae
uellera uirgati custodibant calathisci.
haec tum clarisona pellentes uellera uoce
talia diuino fuderunt carmine fata,
carmine, perfidiae quod post nulla arguet aetas.

    o decus eximium magnis uirtutibus augens,
Emathiae tutamen, opis carissime nato,

The tallest cypress and the nodding plane
And Phaëthon's frail sisters, whose great pain
Occasioned by their brother's fall had changed
Them into poplars. All were so arranged
That they would grow to shade the palace gate.
Prometheus then follows, he whose fate
It was to be bound to a cliff with chains,
His fading scars remind us of his pains.
The gods' own king, his wife and sons were there
But Phoebus and Diana did not care
To come from heaven to congratulate
The couple for their hearts were filled with hate.
    At last when all the guests reclined upon
White couches, tables were brought out, and on
Them dainties were piled high; meanwhile one heard
The song sung by the palsied Fates whose word
Disclosed the future. See their trembling, slight,
Old bodies clothed in robes of purest white
With purple hems. Their snow white heads are bound
With bright red fillets; gnarled hands deftly found
Their never ending task. Their left hands clasped
A distaff clothed in wool, while right hands grasped
It firmly, shaped it into thread; with thumb
They twirled their balanced spindles, made them hum.
And with their teeth they evened out the thread
So flecks of wool clung to their lips instead
Of clinging to the yarn. The snow white wool
Was piled in osier baskets, bulging, full
Before their feet. Then as they worked, their song
Of fate arose in voices, clear and strong,
And all of time will never prove it wrong:
Oh most courageous master, Peleus,
The bulwark of Emathia, your fame
Rests in a son yet to be born, now claim

accipe, quod laeta tibi pandunt luce sorores,
ueridicum oraclum: sed uos, quae fata sequuntur,
    currite ducentes subtegmina, currite, fusi.
adueniet tibi iam portans optata maritis
Hesperus, adueniet fausto cum sidere coniunx,
quae tibi flexanimo mentem perfundat amore,
languidulosque paret tecum coniungere somnos,
leuia substernens robusto brachia collo.
    currite ducentes subtegmina, currite, fusi.
nulla domus tales umquam contexit amores,
nullus amor tali coniunxit foedere amantes,
qualis adest Thetidi, qualis concordia Peleo.
    currite ducentes subtegmina, currite, fusi.
nascetur uobis expers terroris Achilles,
hostibus haud tergo, sed forti pectore notus,
qui persaepe uago uictor certamine cursus
flammea praeuertet celeris uestigia ceruae.
    currite ducentes subtegmina, currite, fusi.
non illi quisquam bello se conferet heros,
cum Phrygii Teucro manabunt sanguine campi,
Troicaque obsidens longinquo moenia bello,
periuri Pelopis uastabit tertius heres.
    currite ducentes subtegmina, currite, fusi.
illius egregias uirtutes claraque facta
saepe fatebuntur gnatorum in funere matres,
cum incultum cano soluent a uertice crinem,
putridaque infirmis uariabunt pectora palmis.
    currite ducentes subtegmina, currite, fusi.
namque uelut densas praecerpens messor aristas
sole sub ardenti flauentia demetit arua,
Troiugenum infesto prosternet corpora ferro.
    currite ducentes subtegmina, currite, fusi.
testis erit magnis uirtutibus unda Scamandri,
quae passim rapido diffunditur Hellesponto,

Your prophecy this happy day from us,
    Run spindles, draw the fatal thread.
Soon Hesperus will rise for you and bring
Into your arms the wife that you desire,
Who will be joined to you and know the fire
Of your embrace before you sleep. So sing
    Out spindles, draw the fatal thread.
No house on earth has known such love before
No lovers were so closely bound together
As Peleus and Thetis to each other.
In harmony they'll love forevermore.
    Turn spindles, draw the fatal thread.
From you shall spring a mighty son whose name
Will be Achilles. He will never flee
The foe, and none will be as swift as he,
A match for dashing hinds as fleet as flame.
    Run spindles, draw the fatal thread.
And no one will dare challenge him in war
When Trojan blood dyes Phrygian field with red
And Pelops' heir will vaunt amid the dead
When he has toppled Troy. Forevermore,
    Turn spindles, draw the fatal thread.
The hero's valor will be known to old
And grieving mothers as they loose their hair
And beating withered breasts, they. pause to stare
At bodies of their sons, so bloodless, cold.
    Turn spindles, draw the fatal thread.
For as the farmer reaps rich sheaves of grain
In golden fields beneath the burning sun,
So shall he smite each Trojan mother's son
With sword that glories in its blood red stain.
    Turn spindles, draw the fatal thread.
Scamander's delta at the Hellespont
Will witness his great valor; all those slain

cuius iter caesis angustans corporum aceruis
alta tepefaciet permixta flumina caede.

currite ducentes subtegmina, currite, fusi.
denique testis erit morti quoque reddita praeda,
cum teres excelso coaceruatum aggere bustum
excipiet niueos perculsae uirginis artus.

currite ducentes subtegmina, currite, fusi.
nam simul ac fessis dederit fors copiam Achiuis
urbis Dardaniae Neptunia soluere uincla,
alta Polyxenia madefient caede sepulcra;
quae, uelut ancipiti succumbens uictima ferro,
proiciet truncum summisso poplite corpus.

currite ducentes subtegmina, currite, fusi.
quare agite optatos animi coniungite amores.
accipiat coniunx felici foedere diuam,
dedatur cupido iam dudum nupta marito.

currite ducentes subtegmina, currite, fusi.
non illam nutrix orienti luce reuisens
hesterno collum poterit circumdare filo,
anxia nec mater discordis maesta puellae
secubitu caros mittet sperare nepotes.

currite ducentes subtegmina, currite, fusi.
talia praefantes quondam felicia Pelei
carmina diuino cecinerunt pectore Parcae.
praesentes namque ante domos inuisere castas
heroum, et sese mortali ostendere coetu,
caelicolae nondum spreta pietate solebant.
saepe pater diuum templo in fulgente reuisens,
annua cum festis uenissent sacra diebus,
conspexit terra centum procumbere tauros.
saepe uagus Liber Parnasi uertice summo
Thyiadas effusis euantis crinibus egit,
cum Delphi tota certatim ex urbe ruentes
acciperent laeti diuum fumantibus aris.

Will choke its flow and lend a crimson stain
And greater warmth than ever was its wont.
    Turn spindles, draw the fatal thread.
The final tribute paid to his great ghost
Will be a barrow to receive the slaughter
Of poor Polyxena, old Priam's daughter,
A lovely sacrifice his final boast.
    Turn spindles, draw the fatal thread.
Her blood will drench the ground where he is lain,
When Fortune breaches Neptune's Trojan walls.
A beast receives the axe's stroke and falls,
So she will kneel before the axe, be slain.
    Turn spindles, draw the fatal thread.
So come, unite in love's sweet consummation
Let Theseus now take his goddess bride;
So bring her to her eager husband's side,
And may their life be free from all vexation.
    Turn spindles, draw the fatal thread.
But when her servant comes with early morn,
The mistress will no longer be a maid;
Her mother will no longer be afraid,
Conceiving hopes for children to be born.
    Turn spindles, draw the fatal thread.
Long, long ago the Fates in prophecy
Revealed to Peleus such things to be.
For then the gods would visit mortal men
And enter homes of heroes now and then
Before religion was despised. One might
See Jupiter himself within his bright
Abode receive his yearly offering,
A hundred bulls were slain for heaven's king.
And Bacchus too was often seen in flight
With wild-haired maenads on Parnassus' height,
As he drove them they shouted: "Evoe."

saepe in letifero belli certamine Mauors
aut rapidi Tritonis era aut Rhamnusia uirgo
armatas hominum est praesens hortata cateruas.
sed postquam tellus scelere est imbuta nefando
iustitiamque omnes cupida de mente fugarunt,
perfudere manus fraterno sanguine fratres,
destitit extinctos gnatus lugere parentes,
optauit genitor primaeui funera nati,
liber ut innuptae poteretur flore nouercae,
ignaro mater substernens se impia nato
impia non uerita est diuos scelerare penates.
omnia fanda nefanda malo permixta furore
iustificam nobis mentem auertere deorum.
quare nec talis dignantur uisere coetus,
nec se contingi patiuntur lumine claro.

LXV

Etsi me assiduo confectum cura dolore
    seuocat a doctis, Ortale, uirginibus,
nec potis est dulcis Musarum expromere fetus
    mens animi, tantis fluctuat ipsa malis—
namque mei nuper Lethaeo gurgite fratris
    pallidulum manans alluit unda pedem,
Troia Rhoeteo quem subter litore tellus
    ereptum nostris obterit ex oculis.

.   .   .   .

numquam ego te, uita frater amabilior,
aspiciam posthac? at certe semper amabo,
    semper maesta tua carmina morte canam,
qualia sub densis ramorum concinit umbris

Delphinians rushed from their town to pay
Him homage on their altars. Mars was seen,
Amid grim warfare; also Triton's queen
Or Nemesis, demanding bravery.
But men soon turned to criminality,
And exiled Justice from their hearts and lands,
Fraternal blood defiled fraternal hands,
The death of parents moved no sons to mourn,
And fathers wished the deaths of their firstborn
In coveting their sons' own promised wives.
A mother lusting for her son contrives
To snare his innocence in incest, prods
Him shamelessly, without regard for gods.
So good and evil were confounded then,
And justice of the gods was turned from men,
Now deities no longer come below
To be with men in daylight's golden glow.

65

I am so worn out by my deep distress
That sorrow, Ortalus, has stilled my song,
Nor can my greatly troubled heart express
The sweet thoughts of the Muses: for not long
Ago my brother set his death-pale foot
Into dark Lethe's flood, and now he lies
Where Trojan earth, Rhoetean shores have put
Their weight on him and hid him from my eyes.

*   *   *   *   *

I'll never see you again, my dearest brother,
Whom I love more than life and always will,
And I shall mourn him, singing, as in other
Times the Daulian bird once sang until

Daulias, absumpti fata gemens Ityli.—
sed tamen in tantis maeroribus, Ortale, mitto
    haec expressa tibi carmina Battiadae,
ne tua dicta uagis nequiquam credita uentis
    effluxisse meo forte putes animo,
ut missum sponsi furtiuo munere malum
    procurrit casto uirginis e gremio,
quod miserae oblitae molli sub ueste locatum,
    dum aduentu matris prosilit, excutitur,
atque illud prono praeceps agitur decursu,
    huic manat tristi conscius ore rubor.

LXVI

Omnia qui magni dispexit lumina mundi,
    qui stellarum ortus comperit atque obitus,
flammeus ut rapidi solis nitor obscuretur,
    ut cedant certis sidera temporibus,
ut Triuiam furtim sub Latmia saxa relegans
    dulcis amor gyro deuocet aerio:
idem me ille Conon caelesti in lumine uidit
    e Bereniceo uertice caesariem
fulgentem clare, quam multis illa dearum
    leuia protendens brachia pollicita est,
qua rex tempestate nouo auctus hymenaeo
    uastatum finis iuerat Assyrios,
dulcia nocturnae portans uestigia rixae,
    quam de uirgineis gesserat exuuiis.
estne nouis nuptis odio Venus? anne parentum
    frustrantur falsis gaudia lacrimulis,
ubertim thalami quas intra limina fundunt?
    non, ita me diui, uera gemunt, iuerint.

The forest rang with grief for Itylus.
Yet, Ortalus, in grieving, I entrust
To you my versions of Callimachus,
So you won't think your words, caught in a gust
Of sudden wind, have been swept from my mind.
Just as an eager lover's gift is sent,
An apple to his secret love, to find
Its hiding place within her bosom, pent
In softness; but her mother suddenly
Entering, frightens her and makes her start;
The apple slips out, bounces, rolling free:
And flushed cheeks show the guilt of her pounding heart.

66

The great star gazer, Conon, he who knew
The splendors of the sky, its secrets too,
The movements of the planets, how the bright
Sun's blaze endures eclipse, how each star's light
Recedes at certain seasons, how sweet love
Calls Trivia from airy paths above,
Confining her within the hollow rock
Of Latmus, Conon knew I was the lock
Of Berenice's hair he saw on high;
Shorn from her head, I now shine in the sky.
She vowed me to the goddesses in prayers
With graceful arms upraised; her king now bears
The traces of his love's sweet consummation;
His nightlong bout now won, he led his nation
To lay waste proud Assyrian frontiers.
Do brides, pretending hate for love, shed tears,
Give happy parents cause for great dismay
By endless weeping on their wedding day?

id mea me multis docuit regina querellis
  inuisente nouo proelia torua uiro.
et tu non orbum luxti deserta cubile,
  sed fratris cari flebile discidium?
quam penitus maestas exedit cura medullas!
  ut tibi tunc toto pectore sollicitae
sensibus ereptis mens excidit! at te ego certe
  cognoram a parua uirgine magnanimam.
anne bonum oblita es facinus, quo regium adepta es
  coniugium, quod non fortior ausit alis?
sed tum maesta uirum mittens quae uerba locuta es!
  Iuppiter, ut tristi lumina saepe manu!
quis te mutauit tantus deus? an quod amantes
  non longe a caro corpore abesse uolunt?
atque ibi me cunctis pro dulci coniuge diuis
  non sine taurino sanguine pollicita es,
si reditum tetulisset. is haut in tempore longo
  captam Asiam Aegypti finibus addiderat.
quis ego pro factis caelesti reddita coetu
  pristina uota nouo munere dissoluo.
inuita, o regina, tuo de uertice cessi,
  inuita: adiuro teque tuumque caput,
digna ferat quod si quis inaniter adiurarit:
  sed qui se ferro postulet esse parem?
ille quoque euersus mons est, quem maximum in oris
  progenies Thiae clara superuehitur,
cum Medi peperere nouum mare, cumque iuuentus
  per medium classi barbara nauit Athon.
quid facient crines, cum ferro talia cedant?
  Iuppiter, ut Chalybon omne genus pereat,
et qui principio sub terra quaerere uenas
  institit ac ferri stringere duritiem!
abiunctae paulo ante comae mea fata sorores
  lugebant, cum se Memnonis Aethiopis

These tears are false; by all the gods, I know:
My young queen, by her wailing, taught me so,
When her new husband went off to the wars.
You feigned a grief, not as one who abhors
Her lonely bed, but as one rues the sad
Departure of a brother. Grieving had
Consumed your heart, vexed by its endless care;
Your senses failed, your mind sank in despair.
I know the daring which brought you renown:
Recall the splendid crime which won your crown
And marriage too. Who else could do this deed?
How sad your words in wishing him godspeed,
Oh Jupiter! how much you rubbed your eyes!
What god has changed you? Now your lover lies
Far off: is this so hard for you to bear?
Was this why you vowed me, your lock of hair
And blood of bulls to all the gods if he,
Your husband, would return. Then, rapidly,
He added Asia to Egyptian land,
And for his deeds, I'm joined to heaven's band;
By my new presence, I fulfill her vow.
Unwillingly, my queen, I left your brow;
Unwillingly, I swear it by your head,
Your person too; may he who lies instead
Of swearing this oath truly get his due.
Who'll say his strength is that of steel? So too,
The mighty Athos was cut down to size,
Which Thia's son traverses in bright skies;
When Persians channeled through that mountainside,
Their youths then sailed their fleet on that new tide.
If steel can conquer mountains, how can I,
A lock of hair, prevail? May they all die,
The Chalybes and all their race; what's more,
The man who first sought out red iron ore

unigena impellens nutantibus aera pennis
    obtulit Arsinoes Locridos ales equos,
isque per aetherias me tollens auolat umbras
    et Veneris casto collocat in gremio.
ipsa suum Zephyritis eo famulum legarat,
    Graiia Canopitis incola litoribus.
inde Venus uario ne solum in lumine caeli
    ex Ariadnaeis aurea temporibus
fixa corona foret, sed nos quoque fulgeremus
    deuotae flaui uerticis exuuiae,
uuidulam a fluctu cedentem ad templa deum me
    sidus in antiquis diua nouum posuit.
Virginis et saeui contingens namque Leonis
    lumina, Callisto iuncta Lycaoniae,
uertor in occasum, tardum dux ante Booten,
    qui uix sero alto mergitur Oceano.
sed quamquam me nocte premunt uestigia diuum,
    lux autem canae Tethyi restituit,
(pace tua fari hic liceat, Rhamnusia uirgo,
    namque ego non ullo uera timore tegam,
nec si me infestis discerpent sidera dictis,
    condita quin ueri pectoris euoluam)
non his tam laetor rebus, quam me afore semper,
    afore me a dominae uertice discrucior,
quicum ego, dum uirgo quondam fuit omnibus expers
    unguentis, una uilia multa bibi.
nunc uos, optato quas iunxit lumine taeda,
    non prius unanimis corpora coniugibus
tradite nudantes reiecta ueste papillas,
    quam iucunda mihi munera libet onyx,
uester onyx, casto colitis quae iura cubili.
    sed quae se impuro dedit adulterio,
illius a mala dona leuis bibat irrita puluis:
    namque ego ab indignis praemia nulla peto.

Beneath the earth and gave its hardness shape.
My sister locks were grieving at the rape
Which sundered us, when lo! that winged steed,
Black Memnon's brother, caught me; with all speed
His pinions beat the darkness, carried me
To Venus' sacred throne; Arsinoë
Had sent him, she who lives upon the sands
Of Greek Canopus. Venus, then, commands
That I, the promised spoil of flaxen hair
With Ariadne's golden crown should share
The heavens. Drenched by my own tears, I graced
The dwellings of the gods, where Venus placed
Me, shining, a new star amid the old,
Between the Virgin and the Lion, fierce and bold,
And near the Bear; Boötes follows me,
But scarcely dips his foot into the sea.
Yet though the gods tread on these locks each night,
In Tethys' realm I pass the hours of light.
(Oh virgin Nemesis, if you permit,
I shall not hide the truth for fear that it
Shall make the angry stars tear me apart
For telling all that's hidden in my heart.)
Here in my present state, there is no gladness,
For parting from my mistress brings me sadness;
Where once I shared her maiden innocence,
I later drank sweet draught of countless scents.
Now virgins, when the torches will unite
You in your marriage with their longed-for light,
Don't bare your breasts, yield to your man's desire,
But offer, before doffing your attire,
Sweet perfumes to me from your onyx vial,
And enter into wedlock without guile.
But she, who violates her vows in lust
Will find her gift consumed by thirsty dust:

sed magis, o nuptae, semper concordia uestras,
    semper amor sedes incolat assiduus.
tu uero, regina, tuens cum sidera diuam
    placabis festis luminibus Venerem,
unguinis expertem non siris esse tuam me,
    sed potius largis affice muneribus.
sidera corruerint utinam! coma regia fiam,
    proximus Hydrochoi fulgeret Oarion!

LXVII

O dulci iucunda uiro, iucunda parenti,
    salue, teque bona Iuppiter auctet ope,
ianua, quam Balbo dicunt seruisse benigne
    olim, cum sedes ipse senex tenuit,
quamque ferunt rursus gnato seruisse maligne,
    postquam es porrecto facta marita sene.
dic agedum nobis, quare mutata feraris
    in dominum ueterem deseruisse fidem.
"Non (ita Caecilio placeam, cui tradita nunc sum)
    culpa mea est, quamquam dicitur esse mea,
nec peccatum a me quisquam pote dicere quicquam:
    uerum istius populi ianua qui te facit,
qui, quacumque aliquid reperitur non bene factum,
    ad me omnes clamant: ianua, culpa tua est."
Non istuc satis est uno te dicere uerbo,
    sed facere ut quiuis sentiat et uideat.
"Qui possum? nemo quaerit nec scire laborat."
    Nos uolumus: nobis dicere ne dubita.
"Primum igitur, uirgo quod fertur tradita nobis,
    falsum est. non illam uir prior attigerit,
languidior tenera cui pendens sicula beta

I ask no gifts from those defiled by sin.
May harmony and true love swell within
Your homes, new brides, increasing constantly,
And you, my queen, when you look up to see
The stars, and honor Venus with the light
Of marriage, offer me my heart's delight,
Many sweet perfumes. Stars, why hold me fast?
If only I could join my queen at last,
Aquarius could seek Orion's side, as in the past.

67

Hail door, you pleased a father and his son
(May Jupiter reward you!) and they say
You served old Balbus well, who once had run
This house and owned it. Now he's passed away,
His son is not that lucky; you belie
Your trust since they laid out his poor old dad,
And pop's young sprig has married. Tell us why
They say you've changed your ways from good to bad.
"Now look (Caecilius, whose door I am,
You hear?), it's not my fault, although they say
It is, but none can prove it worth a damn,
And you know people like to talk that way;
I'm blamed for everything and they cry, 'Hey,
It's your fault door, when everything's awry.'"
It's not enough to state things quite that way,
Speak plainly so one doesn't think you lie.
"How can I? No one cares or wants to know."
Hold on. I've just now asked, if you recall.
"Well then, the bride came as a virgin, though
That's false, for hubby wasn't first at all;
His dick hung like a wilted beet and so

numquam se mediam sustulit ad tunicam;
sed pater illius gnati uiolasse cubile
    dicitur et miseram conscelerasse domum,
siue quod impia mens caeco flagrabat amore,
    seu quod iners sterili semine natus erat,
et quaerendus is unde foret neruosius illud,
    quod posset zonam soluere uirgineam."
Egregium narras mira pietate parentem,
    qui ipse sui gnati minxerit in gremium.
"Atqui non solum hoc dicit se cognitum habere
    Brixia Cycneae supposita speculae,
flauus quam molli praecurrit flumine Mella,
    Brixia Veronae mater amata meae,
sed de Postumio et Corneli narrat amore,
    cum quibus illa malum fecit adulterium.
dixerit hic aliquis: quid? tu istaec, ianua, nosti,
    cui numquam domini limine abesse licet,
nec populum auscultare, sed hic suffixa tigillo
    tantum operire soles aut aperire domum?
saepe illam audiui furtiua uoce loquentem
    solam cum ancillis haec sua flagitia,
nomine dicentem quos diximus, utpote quae mi
    speraret nec linguam esse nec auriculam.
praeterea addebat quendam, quem dicere nolo
    nomine, ne tollat rubra supercilia.
longus homo est, magnas cui lites intulit olim
    falsum mendaci uentre puerperium."

Could never raise its head. His dad found call
To cuckold sonny, dealt his house a blow
So terrible it brought about its fall.
Either his passions made him stoop that low,
Or since his son just had no juice at all,
And he sure did, then daddy wasn't slow
To loose the virgin's girdle. That took gall."
What a history of love! How fatherly
Of him to shame his son so damnably!
"But then old Brixia can also tell
Some stories; she's the town which lies nearby
The golden stream of Melo, near my well
Beloved Verona. Brixia's not shy,
Tells how my mistress knew Postumius
And played the whore with a Cornelius."
Now, now, some one will say, "But look here, door,
How can you know all this? You always stay
Upon your master's threshold, and what's more,
You can't hear people's gossip, since all day
You open and shut the house." "I've heard her say
This to her maids in whispered torrents, pour
Adventures out, and name her boyfriends; gay
And reckless, how she loved to play the whore!
She thought, no doubt, that I was just a door
And couldn't hear or tell. I won't betray
A third one whom she added to her score
For he will arch red eyebrows. I'll just say
He's tall and fucks around, for which activity
He's famous for a false charge of paternity."

LXVIII

Quod mihi fortuna casuque oppressus acerbo
    conscriptum hoc lacrimis mittis epistolium,
naufragum ut eiectum spumantibus aequoris undis
    subleuem et a mortis limine restituam,
quem neque sancta Venus molli requiescere somno
    desertum in lecto caelibe perpetitur,
nec ueterum dulci scriptorum carmine Musae
    oblectant, cum mens anxia peruigilat:
id gratum est mihi, me quoniam tibi dicis amicum,
    muneraque et Musarum hinc petis et Veneris.
sed tibi ne mea sint ignota incommoda, Manli,
    neu me odisse putes hospitis officium,
accipe, quis merser fortunae fluctibus ipse,
    ne amplius a misero dona beata petas.
tempore quo primum uestis mihi tradita pura est,
    iucundum cum aetas florida uer ageret,
multa satis lusi: non est dea nescia nostri,
    quae dulcem curis miscet amaritiem.
sed totum hoc studium luctu fraterna mihi mors
    abstulit. o misero frater adempte mihi,
tu mea tu moriens fregisti commoda, frater,
    tecum una tota est nostra sepulta domus,
omnia tecum una perierunt gaudia nostra,
    quae tuus in uita dulcis alebat amor.
cuius ego interitu tota de mente fugaui
    haec studia atque omnes delicias animi.
quare, quod scribis Veronae turpe Catullo
    esse, quod hic quisquis de meliore nota
frigida deserto tepefactet membra cubili,
    id, Manli, non est turpe, magis miserum est.
ignosces igitur si, quae mihi luctus ademit,
    haec tibi non tribuo munera, cum nequeo.
nam, quod scriptorum non magna est copia apud me,

68

Though you, so crushed by fortune's bitter ways,
Beg in your tear stained note that I should raise
You from your shipwreck on the battered shore,
And snatch you from the door of death; what's more,
Good Venus does not grant to you, unwed,
Contented sleep upon a lonely bed,
Nor can the Muses give you any peace
With all the sweetest poetry of Greece.
By seeking fruits of my poetic art,
You prove yourself my friend; it warms my heart.
Dear Manlius, that you may not mistake
My present state, nor think that I'd forsake
You, I must tell you that misfortune's seas
Have wrecked me too; I cannot give you ease.
When I, in youth, was clothed in purest white,
Much happiness was mine and I could write
The merriest verse; the goddess spied me then
Who joins sweet bitterness to lives of men.
But grief has ended all such efforts now
My brother's dead. Oh dearest brother, how
I'm lost in your own loss; alas, I see
Our house is buried with you wretchedly,
But while you lived and breathed, it was sustained
By mutual affection. I'm constrained
To banish such thoughts from my grieving mind,
With all the pleasures that I used to find.
So when you write, "Catullus, why do you
Stay at Verona, when out here a crew
Of high-class guys all find a warm caress
Within the bed you left behind"; I guess
It's just too bad, but I don't care; and then
I am too grieved to try to help you when
I cannot. I've few authors here at hand

    hoc fit, quod Romae uiuimus: illa domus,
illa mhi sedes, illic mea carpitur aetas;
    huc una ex multis capsula me sequitur.
quod cum ita sit, nolim statuas nos mente maligna
    id facere aut animo non satis ingenuo,
quod tibi non utriusque petenti copia parta est:
    ultro ego deferrem, copia siqua foret.

    LXVIIIA
Non possum reticere, deae, qua me Allius in re
    iuuerit aut quantis iuuerit officiis,
ne fugiens saeclis obliuiscentibus aetas
    illius hoc caeca nocte tegat studium:
sed dicam uobis, uos porro dicite multis
    milibus et facite haec carta loquatur anus.

    .   .   .   .

    notescatque magis mortuus atque magis,
nec tenuem texens sublimis aranea telam
    in deserto Alli nomine opus faciat.
nam, mihi quam dederit duplex Amathusia curam,
    scitis, et in quo me torruerit genere,
cum tantum arderem quantum Trinacria rupes
    lymphaque in Oetaeis Malia Thermopylis,
maesta neque assiduo tabescere lumina fletu
    cessarent tristique imbre madere genae.
qualis in aerii perlucens uertice montis
    riuus muscoso prosilit e lapide,
qui cum de prona praeceps est ualle uolutus,
    per medium densi transit iter populi,
dulce uiatori lasso in sudore leuamen,
    cum grauis exustos aestus hiulcat agros,
ac uelut in nigro iactatis turbine nautis

Because I live at Rome, you understand,
That's my abode and there my life is spent.
I bring a small box here; few things are sent
Along to me, and so you must not judge
Me harshly; it's not that I will not budge
Or that I'm stingy. I would love to send
Some poems, in affection, to my friend.

68A

Oh Muses, I'll no longer hold my peace;
I'll praise dear Allius and never cease
To bear in mind his help to me. Thus I
Must speak, or time may quickly pass him by
And veil his zeal in blind, forgetful night.
So may the ages know what I now write.

    *   *   *   *   *

And may he, through my verse, gain wide renown
Which death and time are powerless to drown,
So that the spider can't obscure the fame
Of Allius with webs that hide his name.
That I've been burned, put through a living hell
By Venus' treachery, you know this well;
Like Etna's molten rocks, seethed terribly
And boiled like waters of Thermopylae;
Tears ran in ceaseless floods from my sad eyes
And drenched my cheeks; just as the rills arise
And leap forth brightly on a mountainside
Between the moss-grown rocks and, gushing, glide
Headlong down a valley, passing through
A throng of busy townsfolk, to renew
The weary traveler's strength, when sultry heat
Cracks parching fields. Just as poor sailors meet

        lenius aspirans aura secunda uenit
iam prece Pollucis, iam Castoris implorata,
        tale fuit nobis Allius auxilium.
is clausum lato patefecit limite campum,
        isque domum nobis isque dedit dominae,
ad quam communes exerceremus amores.
        quo mea se molli candida diua pede
intulit et trito fulgentem in limine plantam
        innixa arguta constituit solea,
coniugis ut quondam flagrans aduenit amore
        Protesilaeam Laodamia domum
inceptam frustra, nondum cum sanguine sacro
        hostia caelestis pacificasset eros.
nil mihi tam ualde placeat, Rhamnusia uirgo,
        quod temere inuitis suscipiatur eris.
quam ieiuna pium desideret ara cruorem,
        docta est amisso Laodamia uiro,
coniugis ante coacta noui dimittere collum,
        quam ueniens una atque altera rursus hiems
noctibus in longis auidum saturasset amorem,
        posset ut abrupto uiuere coniugio,
quod scibant Parcae non longo tempore abesse,
        si miles muros isset ad Iliacos.
nam tum Helenae raptu primores Argiuorum
        coeperat ad sese Troia ciere uiros,
Troia (nefas!) commune sepulcrum Asiae Europaeque,
        Troia uirum et uirtutum omnium acerba cinis,
quaene etiam nostro letum miserabile fratri
        attulit. ei misero frater adempte mihi,
ei misero fratri iucundum lumen ademptum,
        tecum una tota est nostra sepulta domus,
omnia tecum una perierunt gaudia nostra,
        quae tuus in uita dulcis alebat amor.
quem nunc tam longe non inter nota sepulcra

A welcome breeze when blackest squalls had made
Them pray to Castor, Pollux too, for aid,
Such was the help that Allius gave me;
He was my friend in dire necessity,
And opened up the gate to his closed field
And led me to a house where we might yield,
Both my sweet love and I, to passion's fire.
My mistress came with dainty step; desire
Had made her press her shining foot within
The polished threshold, just as once there'd been
A queen who loved the man whom she had wed
Who should have feared him and his house instead,
For sacrifice in it had not been given,
Propitiating all the lords of heaven.
May nothing please me, O Rhamnusian maid,
Which lacks the gods' approval or their aid.
Queen Laodamia then paid the price
One pays for such neglected sacrifice:
Her husband died, was torn from her sweet breast
Before they'd shared two winters in their nest.
Throughout her life she might have tasted of
The fruits of marriage till, too old for love,
She'd then have had her fill. Instead this boy
Was fated to die in far-off, bloody Troy.
For then, because of Helen's rape, the Greek
Lords went to Ilium, as if to seek
A grave for Europe and for Asia too,
And death for heroes and for those they slew.
My brother died close by the Trojan wall;
Alas, my joys are gone beyond recall;
Lost to your brother, taken from my eyes,
With you our house is buried; your demise
Has ended all the love you had for me.
For far off from your home and family,

nec prope cognatos compositum cineres,
sed Troia obscena, Troia infelice sepultum
　　detinet extremo terra aliena solo.
ad quam tum properans fertur simul undique pubes
　　Graeca penetralis deseruisse focos,
ne Paris abducta gauisus libera moecha
　　otia pacato degeret in thalamo.
quo tibi tum casu, pulcerrima Laodamia,
　　ereptum est uita dulcius atque anima
coniugium: tanto te absorbens uertice amoris
　　aestus in abruptum detulerat barathrum,
quale ferunt Grai Pheneum prope Cyllenaeum
　　siccare emulsa pingue palude solum,
quod quondam caesis montis fodisse medullis
　　audit falsiparens Amphitryoniades,
tempore quo certa Stymphalia monstra sagitta
　　perculit imperio deterioris eri,
pluribus ut caeli tereretur ianua diuis,
　　Hebe nec longa uirginitate foret.
sed tuus altus amor barathro fuit altior illo,
　　qui tamen indomitam ferre iugum docuit.
nam nec tam carum confecto aetate parenti
　　una caput seri nata nepotis alit,
qui, cum diuitiis uix tandem inuentus auitis
　　nomen testatas intulit in tabulas,
impia derisi gentilis gaudia tollens
　　suscitat a cano uolturium capiti:
nec tantum niueo gauisa est ulla columbo
　　compar, quae multo dicitur improbius
oscula mordenti semper decerpere rostro,
　　quam quae praecipue multiuola est mulier.
sed tu horum magnos uicisti sola furores,
　　ut semel es flauo conciliata uiro.
aut nihil aut paulo cui tum concedere digna

Entombed alone beneath a foreign sky
In hated and accursed Troy you lie.
To this town all the youth of Greece once came
Leaving their homes so Paris could not shame
Them by enjoying with impunity
His stolen harlot in tranquillity.
Fair Laodamia, in that foul strife,
Your most beloved husband lost his life.
Love's vortex flung you headlong to its core
And swirled you downward. As in Grecian lore,
The town, Pheneus, losing much rich soil,
Had its swamps drained by Hercules' great toil;
It's said that he scooped out the mountainside,
Obeyed a mortal master, won his bride
When he destroyed Stymphalian birds with bow
And arrows so that heaven's gates would know
Him as a god and that chaste Hebe might
Be his. But Laodamia, your plight
Was eased by your true love, so pure and good
Which helped you bear the yoke of widowhood.
Old age holds nothing quite so dear for one
As when an only daughter bears a son,
Whose name is quickly entered on the will
With witnesses as granddad wields the quill.
This ends the greedy glee of kin; instead
Those vultures are scared off from that gray head.
No dove was ever so delighted by
Her snow white mate who's said to satisfy
Her only when he lets himself be torn
By her fierce bill. No woman yet was born
To match the lustful nature of the dove,
But you soon proved yourself its match in love,
Once you were wedded to your fair-haired king.
My sweetheart rivaled you in everything

      lux mea se nostrum contulit in gremium,
quam circumcursans hinc illinc saepe Cupido
      fulgebat crocina candidus in tunica.
quae tamen etsi uno non est contenta Catullo,
      rara uerecundae furta feremus erae,
ne nimium simus stultorum more molesti.
      saepe etiam Iuno, maxima caelicolum,
coniugis in culpa flagrantem concoquit iram,
      noscens omniuoli plurima furta Iouis.
atqui nec diuis homines componier aequum est,

.   .   .   .

.   .   .   .

      ingratum tremuli tolle parentis onus.
nec tamen illa mihi dextra deducta paterna
      fragrantem Assyrio uenit odore domum,
sed furtiua dedit mira munuscula nocte,
      ipsius ex ipso dempta uiri gremio.
quare illud satis est, si nobis is datur unis
      quem lapide illa dies candidiore notat.

hoc tibi, quod potui, confectum carmine munus
      pro multis, Alli, redditur officiis,
ne uestrum scabra tangat rubigine nomen
      haec atque illa dies atque alia atque alia.
huc addent diui quam plurima, quae Themis olim
      antiquis solita est munera ferre piis.
sitis felices et tu simul et tua uita,
      et domus ipsa in qua lusimus et domina,
et qui principio nobis te tradidit auctor,
      a quo sunt primo omnia nata bona,
et longe ante omnes mihi quae me carior ipso est,
      lux mea, qua uiua uiuere dulce mihi est.

Of love; she laid her heart upon my heart,
While Cupid ranged about and poised his dart,
Gleaming in his bright cloak of saffron hue.
Catullus, she's had flings with others too,
So you'll condone a little indiscretion
Lest, like a fool, you make it an obsession.
As Juno, queen of our divinities
Can overlook Jove's infidelities,
Although his sins are well within her ken.
But since one can't compare the gods to men

    .   .   .   .

    .   .   .   .

Dispel a palsied father's grave alarm.
She was no bride with hand on daddy's arm,
Led to my house sweet with its Syrian scent,
But in a fabulous night of bliss she lent
Me favors smuggled from her husband's bed.
So now I am contented since she's said
That mine alone's the day she marks in red.

So I send you this gift of poetry,
Dear Allius, for kindness shown to me,
So that the passing years will not encrust,
Corrode your name with all-consuming rust.
And may the gods grant you the greatest store
Of gifts which Themis offered men of yore:
May you and your true love live blessedly
In this, your house, which gave my girl and me
Its shelter for our burning love. God bless
The man who first assured our happiness
By bringing us together, dearest heart,
More precious to me than my life and art.

LXIX

Noli admirari, quare tibi femina nulla,
    Rufe, uelit tenerum supposuisse femur,
non si illam rarae labefactes munere uestis
    aut perluciduli deliciis lapidis.
laedit te quaedam mala fabula, qua tibi fertur
    ualle sub alarum trux habitare caper.
hunc metuunt omnes, neque mirum: nam mala ualde est
    bestia, nec quicum bella puella cubet.
quare aut crudelem nasorum interfice pestem,
    aut admirari desine cur fugiunt.

LXX

Nulli se dicit mulier mea nubere malle
    quam mihi, non si se Iuppiter ipse petat.
dicit: sed mulier cupido quod dicit amanti,
    in uento et rapida scribere oportet aqua.

LXXI

Si cui iure bono sacer alarum obstitit hircus,
    aut si quem merito tarda podagra secat,
aemulus iste tuus, qui uestrum exercet amorem,
    mirifice est a te nactus utrumque malum.
nam quotiens futuit, totiens ulciscitur ambos:
    illam affligit odore, ipse perit podagra.

69

Rufus, no one is amazed that you
Can't get a girl to spread her tender thighs,
Not even if you give her gifts of new
Expensive clothing, jewels of great size,
Translucent, lovely. I have heard it said
That in your armpit you've a grisly guest,
A reeking he-goat. No babe goes to bed
With such an evil beast: all fear this pest.
You've got to stop your stinking or be done
With wondering why they take one whiff and run.

70 - change ?

My love says she would marry only me,
And Jove himself could never make her care.
What women say to lovers, you'll agree,
One writes on running water or on air.

71

If ever a man deserved the gout,
Or stunk like a goat to pay for sin,
Your rival's the guy; the guilty lout
Makes love in your bed; when he gets in
He stinks like hell; she passes out,
While he groans curses, half-dead with the gout.

LXXII

Dicebas quondam solum te nosse Catullum,
    Lesbia, nec prae me uelle tenere Iouem.
dilexi tum te non tantum ut uulgus amicam,
    sed pater ut gnatos diligit et generos.
nunc te cognoui: quare etsi impensius uror,
    multo mi tamen es uilior et leuior.
qui potis est, inquis? quod amantem iniuria talis
    cogit amare magis, sed bene uelle minus.

LXXIII

Desine de quoquam quicquam bene uelle mereri
    aut aliquem fieri posse putare pium.
omnia sunt ingrata, nihil fecisse benigne
    immo etiam taedet, taedet obestque magis;
ut mihi, quem nemo grauius nec acerbius urget,
    quam modo qui me unum atque unicum amicum habuit.

LXXIV

Gellius audierat patruum obiurgare solere,
    si quis delicias diceret aut faceret.
hoc ne ipsi accideret, patrui perdepsuit ipsam
    uxorem et patruum reddidit Harpocratem.
quod uoluit fecit: nam, quamuis irrumet ipsum
    nunc patruum, uerbum non faciet patruus.

72 despair

Lesbia, you often used to dare
To claim you'd take Catullus over Jove;
I loved you then, not as those men who rove
In search of whores, but as good fathers care
For sons and daughters. Though I now desire
You more than I did once, you are less dear
Since you're proved trashy. "How is this?" you jeer.
Because I am so injured, I'm on fire,
Both sad and anguished, and I must confess
It makes me want you more, but like you less.

73

Give up all hope of anything from anyone,
Give up the expectation of men's piety;
There is no gratitude for any kindness done.
Oh gods, it's tedious, as more and more I see
How in my case, I am betrayed most bitterly
By him who called me his dear friend, his only one.

74

Gellius heard his uncle used to rant
At all who spoke of sex or liked their lay,
Lest this should be his lot, he ploughed his aunt,
Shut uncle up completely in this way.
He fixed him good; even if he should screw
Uncle himself, that guy would not say boo.

LXXV

Huc est mens deducta tua mea, Lesbia, culpa
    atque ita se officio perdidit ipsa suo,
ut iam nec bene uelle queat tibi, si optima fias,
    nec desistere amare, omnia si facias.

LXXVI

Siqua recordanti benefacta priora uoluptas
    est homini, cum se cogitat esse pium,
nec sanctam uiolasse fidem, nec foedere nullo
    diuum ad fallendos numine abusum homines,
multa parata manent in longa aetate, Catulle,
    ex hoc ingrato gaudia amore tibi.
nam quaecumque homines bene cuiquam aut dicere possunt
    aut facere, haec a te dictaque factaque sunt.
omnia quae ingratae perierunt credita menti.
    quare iam te cur amplius excrucies?
quin tu animo offirmas atque istinc teque reducis,
    et dis inuitis desinis esse miser?
difficile est longum subito deponere amorem,
    difficile est, uerum hoc qua lubet efficias:
una salus haec est, hoc est tibi peruincendum,
    hoc facias, siue id non pote siue pote.
o di, si uestrum est misereri, aut si quibus umquam
    extremam iam ipsa in morte tulistis opem,
me miserum aspicite et, si uitam puriter egi,
    eripite hanc pestem perniciemque mihi,
quae mihi subrepens imos ut torpor in artus
    expulit ex omni pectore laetitias.
non iam illud quaero, contra me ut diligat illa,
    aut, quod non potis est, esse pudica uelit:
ipse ualere opto et taetrum hunc deponere morbum.
    o di, reddite mi hoc pro pietate mea.

75

Your ways, my Lesbia, have led my heart astray,
Made it destroy itself through love for you;
I'd hate you though you were a saint in every way,
But I keep longing for you still, no matter what you do.

76

If one, remembering his piety,
His kindly deeds, who thinks that he's been just,
Has kept his word, has had no cause to be
A liar, heedless of his sacred trust,
Catullus, you'll have years of happiness
To pay you for this thankless love you've known;
What men can say or do in kindliness,
You've surely said and done, but it's all blown
Away, means nothing to this thankless soul,
So why grieve more at what no grief will heal,
Why not be firm and find another goal?
The gods don't will this misery you feel.
Yet it's so hard to cast one's love aside.
It is not easy but you must prevail;
It's your sole hope. It cannot be denied
You must win out though you're afraid you'll fail.
Oh gods, if you know pity, if you give
Help to one who's dying, then help me;
If I've lived purely, grant that I may live
Freed of this plague and all my misery.
Alas, this numbness creeping through my flesh
Expels all hope of happiness of heart.
I don't ask her to give me love afresh,
In unaccustomed virtue make a start:
I only ask that I be well, be free,
Oh gods, let this reward my piety.

LXXVII

Rufe mihi frustra ac nequiquam credite amice
    (frustra? immo magno cum pretio atque malo),
sicine subrepsti mi, atque intestina perurens
    ei misero eripuisti omnia nostra bona?
eripuisti, heu heu nostrae crudele uenenum
    uitae, heu heu nostrae pestis amicitiae.

LXXVIII

Gallus habet fratres, quorum est lepidissima coniunx
    alterius, lepidus filius alterius.
Gallus homo est bellus; nam dulces iungit amores,
    cum puero ut bello bella puella cubet.
Gallus homo est stultus, nec se uidet esse maritum,
    qui patruus patrui monstret adulterium.

LXXVIIIA

   *   *   *   *   *   *   *   *

sed nunc id doleo, quod purae pura puellae
    suauia comminxit spurca saliua tua.
uerum id non impune feres: nam te omnia saecla
    noscent et, qui sis, fama loquetur anus.

LXXIX

Lesbius est pulcer. quid ni? quem Lesbia malit
    quam te cum tota gente, Catulle, tua.
sed tamen hic pulcer uendat cum gente Catullum,
    si tria notorum suauia reppererit.

77

Rufus, I trusted you and was your friend,
And was your friend in vain, or at a cost
So ruinous that I could not defend
My heart against you; wretched, lost,
It festers, and a poisoned creature, I
Know sadly that your friendship was a lie.

78

Gallus has two brothers. One's possessed
Of a most charming wife, the other's blessed
With a most charming son, and Gallus brings
The two together, helps the charming things
To bed. But Gallus, the big fool, should not forget,
His nephew has become his biggest threat.

78A
*   *   *   *   *

But what bugs me is that your nasty spit
Has touched a virgin girl upon the lip;
But you'll not have it free: You are a shit
With whom each age shall have acquaintanceship.

79

Lesbius is pretty. Shouldn't she,
Our Lesbia, prefer him then to you,
Catullus? But if he can find just three
Good friends, then let him sell me, all my kinfolk too.

LXXX

Quid dicam, Gelli, quare rosea ista labella
    hiberna fiant candidiora niue,
mane domo cum exis et cum te octaua quiete
    e molli longo suscitat hora die?
nescio quid certe est: an uere fama susurrat
    grandia te medii tenta uorare uiri?
sic certe est: clamant Victoris rupta miselli
    ilia, et emulso labra notata sero.

LXXXI

Nemone in tanto potuit populo esse, Iuuenti,
    bellus homo, quem tu diligere inciperes,
praeterquam iste tuus moribunda ab sede Pisauri
    hospes inaurata pallidior statua,
qui tibi nunc cordi est, quem tu praeponere nobis
    audes, et nescis quod facinus facias?

LXXXII

Quinti, si tibi uis oculos debere Catullum
    aut aliud si quid carius est oculis,
eripere ei noli, multo quod carius illi
    est oculis seu quid carius est oculis.

80

Gellius, why are your lips white as snow,
Which should be red, when you get up at dawn,
Or when you've had your midday nap and go
Out of your house? Those stories told in scorn
Show something's wrong; is that a truthful tale
That sucking cock is what you love to do?
Poor Victor's busted balls show why you're pale,
Your lips as well, smeared with his milked-out goo.

81

Juventius, how could you think our land
Had none so handsome, and how could this creep
Who's bloodless as a statue seem so grand,
When he's from old Pisaurum, that junk heap?
And now you dare to choose him over me,
Your crime has consequences you don't see.

82

If you wish him to owe you both his eyes,
Or more, then Quintius, don't take away
Catullus' treasure, his most valued prize,
Which he deems dearer than his very eyes.

LXXXIII

Lesbia mi praesente uiro mala plurima dicit:
    haec illi fatuo maxima laetitia est.
mule, nihil sentis? si nostri oblita taceret,
    sana esset: nunc quod gannit et obloquitur,
non solum meminit, sed, quae multo acrior est res,
    irata est. hoc est, uritur et loquitur.

LXXXIV

Chommoda dicebat, si quando commoda uellet
    dicere, et insidias Arrius hinsidias,
et tum mirifice sperabat se esse locutum,
    cum quantum poterat dixerat hinsidias.
credo, sic mater, sic liber auunculus eius,
    sic maternus auus dixerat atque auia.
hoc misso in Syriam requierant omnibus aures:
    audibant eadem haec leniter et leuiter,
nec sibi postilla metuebant talia uerba,
    cum subito affertur nuntius horribilis,
Ionios fluctus, postquam illuc Arrius isset,
    iam non Ionios esse sed Hionios.

LXXXV

Odi et amo. quare id faciam, fortasse requiris?
    nescio, sed fieri sentio et excrucior.

6 hope

83

Lesbia has a husband; speaks of me
In scorn, at which her hopeless dolt is gay.
This mule knows nothing. If she had no say
About me, he'd be safer then, for she,
By railing recollects, and feels her sore.
Her passion grows with speech. Her longing more.

84

Advantage was not what "hadvantage" knew,
And "hambush" ambushed Arrius' speech,
Yet he was certain that his words rang true
Because he "hambushed" loudly. Each to each,
His mother, ex-slave uncle "hambushed" thus,
Thus too his mama's pappa and his wife.
So when he went to Syria, all of us
Unplugged our ears, words sounded smooth, our life
No longer was harassed by such vile speech;
Then bad news came from seas Ionian,
For Arrius upon a far-off beach
Loudly proclaimed that they were now "Hionian."

85

I hate and love. You ask, "How can this be?"
God knows! What wretchedness! What loathsome misery!

LXXXVI

Quintia formosa est multis. mihi candida, longa,
    recta est: haec ego sic singula confiteor.
totum illud formosa nego: nam nulla uenustas,
    nulla in tam magno est corpore mica salis.
Lesbia formosa est, quae cum pulcerrima tota est,
    tum omnibus una omnis surripuit Veneres.

LXXXVII

Nulla potest mulier tantum se dicere amatam
    uere, quantum a me Lesbia amata mea est.
nulla fides ullo fuit umquam foedere tanta,
    quanta in amore tuo ex parte reperta mea est.

LXXXVIII

Quid facit is, Gelli, qui cum matre atque sorore
    prurit et abiectis peruigilat tunicis?
quid facit is, patruum qui non sinit esse maritum?
    ecquid scis quantum suscipiat sceleris?
suscipit, o Gelli, quantum non ultima Tethys
    nec genitor Nympharum abluit Oceanus:
nam nihil est quicquam sceleris, quo prodeat ultra,
    non si demisso se ipse uoret capite.

86 *2*

Yes, Quintia pleases many. I agree
She's tall and fair and straight, as all can see,
But I can't grant her more; she lacks that grace
Which makes for beauty both in form and face.
Now Lesbia has beauty, everything;
She's captured all the graces: these I sing.

87 *3*

What woman truly says she's loved as much
As you, my Lesbia, are loved by me?
What faithfulness in love was ever such
As mine; or offered half so willingly? *compulsion*

88

What's Gellius up to now? He's all night long
With sis and mom in bed, their tunics off.
And doesn't he know he does uncle wrong
By making him a cuckold? We all scoff
At both, but Tethys can't wash out such sin,
Nor Ocean, the nymphs' father; that sick
Fool could not do worse, who revels gaily in
This filth, not even should he stoop, suck his own dick.

LXXXIX

Gellius est tenuis: quid ni? cui tam bona mater
    tamque ualens uiuat tamque uenusta soror
tamque bonus patruus tamque omnia plena puellis
    cognatis, quare is desinat esse macer?
qui ut nihil attingat, nisi quod fas tangere non est,
    quantumuis quare sit macer inuenies.

XC

Nascatur magus ex Gelli matrisque nefando
    coniugio et discat Persicum aruspicium:
nam magus ex matre et gnato gignatur oportet,
    si uera est Persarum impia religio,
gratus ut accepto ueneretur carmine diuos
    omentum in flamma pingue liquefaciens.

XCI

Non ideo, Gelli, sperabam te mihi fidum
    in misero hoc nostro, hoc perdito amore fore,
quod te cognossem bene constantemue putarem
    aut posse a turpi mentem inhibere probro;
sed neque quod matrem nec germanam esse uidebam
    hanc tibi, cuius me magnus edebat amor.
et quamuis tecum multo coniungerer usu,
    non satis id causae credideram esse tibi.
tu satis id duxti: tantum tibi gaudium in omni
    culpa est, in quacumque est aliquid sceleris.

89

Gellius is thin: why not? His mom
Obliges and his charming sister too;
His uncle lets his pretty cousins come
To visit him, and he knows what to do.
His naughty prick is always getting in
Where it should not. No wonder that he's thin.

90

Let Gellius and his mother have a wizard son
Born of their unholy coupling. Persians say
That such foul lovers bear magicians, that's if one
Believes such Persian hocus-pocus; their son may
Appease the gods by singing hymns of praise
And offering entrails in the sacred blaze.

91

Gellius, I didn't think that you
Would wreck my wretched love affair; I knew
You well enough to know you were no friend,
And that your lust for incest had no end;
I saw that she whose love consumed my soul
Was not your sister, mother, hence no goal
Of your well-known incestuous desire.
I never thought our closeness would inspire
You to betray me. Your heart's true delight
Lies in all kinds of vice and willful spite.

XCII

Lesbia mi dicit semper male nec tacet umquam
    de me: Lesbia me dispeream nisi amat.
quo signo? quia sunt totidem mea: deprecor illam
    assidue, uerum dispeream nisi amo.

XCIII

Nil nimium studeo, Caesar, tibi uelle placere,
    nec scire utrum sis albus an ater homo.

XCIV

Mentula moechatur. Moechatur mentula? Certe.
    Hoc est quod dicunt: ipsa olera olla legit.

XCV

Zmyrna mei Cinnae nonam post denique messem
    quam coepta est nonamque edita post hiemem,
milia cum interea quingenta Hortensius uno
    ·   ·   ·   ·   ·   ·   ·   ·
Zmyrna cauas Satrachi penitus mittetur ad undas,
    Zmyrnam cana diu saecula peruoluent.
at Volusi annales Paduam morientur ad ipsam
    et laxas scombris saepe dabunt tunicas.
parua mei mihi sint cordi monimenta
    at populus tumido gaudeat Antimacho.

92

Lesbia bitches at me: how she rails!
But I'll be damned if she does not love me,
For I'm like her. My bitching never fails
Nor my abuse, but love her? Certainly!

93

Caesar, I don't care to be polite,
Don't give a damn if you are black or white.

94

Pricko commits adulteries. Adulteries?
The pot will find its beans and peas.

95

Nine wintertimes since it was first begun
My Cinna's poem "Smyrna" 's now complete;
Hortensius in just one year has done
A half a million lines. But far from Crete,
The "Smyrna" will find readers, ages will
Grow gray in reading it, while soon to die,
The "Annals of Volusius" will still
Find use in wrapping mackerel; thus I
Rejoice in Cinna's modest efforts while
Fools praise Antimachus' windy, pompous style.

XCVI

Si quicquam mutis gratum acceptumue sepulcris
    accidere a nostro, Calue, dolore potest,
quo desiderio ueteres renouamus amores
    atque olim missas flemus amicitias,
certe non tanto mors immatura dolori est
    Quintiliae, quantum gaudet amore tuo.

XCVII

Non (ita me di ament) quicquam referre putaui,
    utrumne os an culum olfacerem Aemilio.
nilo mundius hoc, nihiloque immundius illud,
    uerum etiam culus mundior et melior:
nam sine dentibus est. hoc dentis sesquipedalis,
    gingiuas uero ploxeni habet ueteris,
praeterea rictum qualem diffissus in aestu
    meientis mulae cunnus habere solet.
hic futuit multas et se facit esse uenustum,
    et non pistrino traditur atque asino?
quem siqua attingit, non illam posse putemus
    aegroti culum lingere carnificis?

XCVIII

In te, si in quemquam, dici pote, putide Victi,
    id quod uerbosis dicitur et fatuis.
ista cum lingua, si usus ueniat tibi, possis
    culos et crepidas lingere carpatinas.
si nos omnino uis omnes perdere, Victi,
    hiscas: omnino quod cupis efficies.

96

If, in the silent grave, she still can find
A sweetness in our loneliness and grief,
Dear Calvus, by our longing we may bind
Our loves to us, though we have had to part:
Quintilia may be sad her life was brief,
But happy that she lives on in your heart.

97

I couldn't tell the difference worth a straw,
I swear it, whether I sniffed head or tail
Of that Aemilius; he would overawe
Me either way, but truly now I fail
To find his ass so bad: it has no teeth,
While his mouth's full of choppers. And their shape!
Their length is half a yard, with gums beneath
Like broken wagon frames. They yawn and gape,
The open cunts of pissing mules in heat.
How well he screws, how much his charm and stink
Would suit a slave! The babe he fucks would eat
The rotting ass hole of a dying hangman fink.

98

If anyone deserves what others say
Of windbags, stinky Victius, it's you.
Your tongue would be more useful, any day,
At ass holes, or a ploughman's shitty shoe.
If you would like to kill us, every one,
Yawn, Victius, your stench will get it done.

XCIX

Surripui tibi, dum ludis, mellite Iuuenti,
    suauiolum dulci dulcius ambrosia.
uerum id non impune tuli: namque amplius horam
    suffixum in summa me memini esse cruce,
dum tibi me purgo nec possum fletibus ullis
    tantillum uestrae demere saeuitiae.
nam simul id factum est, multis diluta labella
    guttis abstersisti omnibus articulis,
ne quicquam nostro contractum ex ore maneret,
    tamquam commictae spurca saliua lupae.
praeterea infesto miserum me tradere amori
    non cessasti omnique excruciare modo,
ut mi ex ambrosia mutatum iam fore illud
    suauiolum tristi tristius elleboro.
quam quoniam poenam misero proponis amori,
    numquam iam posthac basia surripiam.

C

Caelius Aufillenum et Quintius Aufillenam
    flos Veronensum depereunt iuuenum,
hic fratrem, ille sororem. hoc est, quod dicitur, illud
    fraternum uere dulce sodalicium.
cui faueam potius? Caeli, tibi: nam tua nobis
    perspecta ex igni est unica amicitia,
cum uesana meas torreret flamma medullas.
    sis felix, Caeli, sis in amore potens.

99

Ah sweet Juventius, I snatched from you
A fleet, ambrosial kiss while you were playing.
Truly I suffered for it, for I knew
An hour upon the rack; there was no paying,
No purge for my rash act. Tears did not halt
Your brutal flood of words, nor mollify
Your rage. Your fingers scrubbed your lips; my fault
Had soiled them past pure water's power, and I
Discovered that my loathsome, leprous touch
Was bad as any filthy, pissed-on whore's;
The pain inflicted by your spite was such
That love had brought me half a thousand sores.
Thus that kiss changed from nectar into gall,
And I into the wretchedest of men,
And since you won't accept my love at all,
I promise not to snatch a kiss again.

100

Caelius for Aufilenus yearns,
And Quintius for Aufilena, too,
One for the brother, one for the sister burns,
Verona's perfect pair. And of this crew
Whom shall I favor then? Caelius, you!
You proved yourself my friend by your good turns
When flames consumed my heart. Since it's your due,
Be happy, Caelius, good luck to you!

CI

Multas per gentes et multa per aequora uectus
    aduenio has miseras, frater, ad inferias,
ut te postremo donarem munere mortis
    et mutam nequiquam alloquerer cinerem.
quandoquidem fortuna mihi tete abstulit ipsum,
    heu miser indigne frater adempte mihi,
nunc tamen interea haec, prisco quae more parentum
    tradita sunt tristi munere ad inferias,
accipe fraterno multum manantia fletu,
    atque in perpetuum, frater, aue atque uale.

CII

Si quicquam tacito commissum est fido ab amico,
    cuius sit penitus nota fides animi,
meque esse inuenies illorum iure sacratum,
    Corneli, et factum me esse puta Harpocratem.

CIII

Aut sodes mihi redde decem sestertia, Silo,
    deinde esto quamuis saeuus et indomitus:
aut, si te nummi delectant, desine quaeso
    leno esse atque idem saeuus et indomitus.

CIV

Credis me potuisse meae maledicere uitae,
    ambobus mihi quae carior est oculis?
non potui, nec, si possem, tam perdite amarem:
    sed tu cum Tappone omnia monstra facis.

101

Through many peoples, over many seas,
I come dear brother, for these obsequies:
I set these gifts beside your grave and speak
To silent ashes. Sadly now I seek
To know why fortune separated two
Joined by their love together, taking you.
And as our fathers' customs bid us bring
The dead their due, accept this offering,
Wet with my tears which, more than words can, tell
My brother hail, forever hail, farewell.

102

If any secret's whispered by a friend,
To one who's known for silent loyalty,
Cornelius, I'm steadfast to this end:
You'll find a mute Harpocrates in me.

103

Look, Silo, if you give me back my dough,
Be wild and vicious as you like, but you
Sure like my money. Well then, don't be so
Wild and vicious when you sell a screw.

104

How could you think that I'd speak ill of her
Who's even dearer to me than my eyes?
I wish I loved her less. As for your slur,
Buffoons like you make things ten times their size.

CV

Mentula conatur Pipleium scandere montem:
    Musae furcillis praecipitem eiciunt.

CVI

Cum puero bello praeconem qui uidet esse,
    quid credat, nisi se uendere discupere?

CVII

Si quicquam cupido optantique optigit umquam
    insperanti, hoc est gratum animo proprie.
quare hoc est gratum nobis quoque carius auro
    quod te restituis, Lesbia, mi cupido.
restituis cupido atque insperanti, ipsa refers te
    nobis. o lucem candidiore nota!
quis me uno uiuit felicior, aut magis hac res
    optandas uita dicere quis poterit?

CVIII

Si, Comini, populi arbitrio tua cana senectus
    spurcata impuris moribus intereat,
non equidem dubito quin primum inimica bonorum
    lingua exsecta auido sit data uulturio,
effossos oculos uoret atro gutture coruus,
    intestina canes, cetera membra lupi.

105

Pricko tries to climb the poet's hill;
The Muses with their pitchforks praise his skill.

106

That pretty boy is with the auctioneers.
Perhaps he wants to sell himself to queers?

107

That which most delights the thoughtful mind
Lies in those things one never hoped to find;
Dear Lesbia, since you've returned to me
Who longed for you, what gold could ever be
So precious? No, I never dared to pray
That you'd come back. Oh bright and happy day!
What living man's as fortunate as I?
Who has such love and knows such joy thereby?

108

Cominius, if you, though old and gray,
Were put to death for all your evil, then
Your tongue, which speaks such ill of decent men,
Would be cut out and flung to birds of prey,
Black-throated crows would gulp your gouged-out eyes,
The dogs your bowels, wolves your breast and thighs.

CIX

Iucundum, mea uita, mihi proponis amorem
    hunc nostrum inter nos perpetuumque fore.
di magni, facite ut uere promittere possit,
    atque id sincere dicat et ex animo,
ut liceat nobis tota perducere uita
    aeternum hoc sanctae foedus amicitiae.

CX

Aufilena, bonae semper laudantur amicae:
    accipiunt pretium, quae facere instituunt.
tu, quod promisti, mihi quod mentita inimica es,
    quod nec das et fers saepe, facis facinus.
aut facere ingenuae est, aut non promisse pudicae,
    Aufilena, fuit: sed data corripere
fraudando officiis, plus quam meretricis auarae,
    quae sese toto corpore prostituit.

CXI

Aufilena, uiro contentam uiuere solo,
    nuptarum laus ex laudibus eximiis:
sed cuiuis quamuis potius succumbere par est,
    quam matrem fratres ex patruo parere.

CXII

Multus homo es, Naso, neque tecum multus homo est qui
    descendit: Naso, multus es et pathicus.

109   hope $

My life, you offer me a love affair
With promises of pleasure which we'll share.
    Great gods, just let her promise truly now
    And let a deep sincerity sustain her vow.
And may we carry out with no vexation
A lifelong treaty of association.

110

Aufilena, kindly ladies are
Well spoken of, they're paid for what they do;
You're not that kind of lady, you fall far
Short of what you've promised, and since you
Must always take and never give, you are
A grasping fraud. If you had been one who
Said no, you'd have been chaste, but you've grabbed more
For less than the most greedy, filthy whore.

111

Aufilena, if one lives content
With just one husband, this is excellent.
But better screw with all than be the mother
Of your own cousins by your father's brother.

112

Few men make friends with Naso, I'm afraid.
The friends he makes are those by whom he's made.

CXIII

Consule Pompeio primum duo, Cinna, solebant
    Maeciliam: facto consule nunc iterum
manserunt duo, sed creuerunt milia in unum
    singula. fecundum semen adulterio.

CXIV

Firmano saltu non falso Mentula diues
    fertur, qui tot res in se habet egregias,
aucupium omne genus, piscis, prata, arua ferasque.
    nequiquam: fructus sumptibus exsuperat.
quare concedo sit diues, dum omnia desint.
    saltum laudemus, dum domo ipse egeat.

CXV

Mentula habet instar triginta iugera prati,
    quadraginta arui: cetera sunt maria.
cur non diuitiis Croesum superare potis sit,
    uno qui in saltu tot bona possideat,
prata arua ingentes siluas saltusque paludesque
    usque ad Hyperboreos et mare ad Oceanum?
omnia magna haec sunt, tamen ipsest maximus ultro,
    non homo, sed uero mentula magna minax.

113

Cinna, in Pompey's consulship, our own
Maecilia was kept by only two.
He's consul once again: that pair has grown
A thousandfold. That's what adultery can do!

114

Yes, it is truly said that Pricko's rich;
In Firmum he possesses such lush land
With its broad acres, game at every hand,
And fowl and fish and pasture, cornlands which
Are fertile, yet he's wasted all; the louse
Is broke. But still let's praise his fertile land,
It's all we can do for he lacks a house.

115

Thirty acres, Pricko, you reserve
As meadow, forty's for the plough; observe
That all the rest is swamp. Now this estate
Would shame old Croesus, for you shut your gate
On billions with your meadows, forests, fens,
To Ocean and the Hyperboreans.
But all you own, compared to you, looks sick,
You're such a pompous, ponderous, proud prick.

CXVI

Saepe tibi studioso animo uenante requirens
    carmina uti possem mittere Battiadae,
qui te lenirem nobis, neu conarere
    tela infesta mihi mittere in usque caput,
hunc uideo mihi nunc frustra sumptum esse laborem,
    Gelli, nec nostras hic ualuisse preces.
contra nos tela ista tua euitabimus amictu
    at fixus nostris tu dabis supplicium.

116

I've often cast about how I might send
The poems of Callimachus, a gift
By which you'd be appeased, and so might end
Our war of words, but since you want our rift
Maintained, then Gellius, it's all in vain.
Now in return, I'll parry your attack,
I'll wrap my cloak about my arm and rain
Darts down on you, and really pay you back.

GLOSSARY

Many proper names which appear in the text of Catullus have been omitted here because they are otherwise unidentifiable.

Aeëtes   King of Colchis and father of Medea. He had killed Phrixus, a Theban prince who had come to his realm on a golden ram. The Argonauts later made an expedition to Colchis to regain its fleece. (Poem 64)

Aegeus   King of Athens and father of Theseus. Thinking Theseus had been killed by the Minotaur in Crete, he hurled himself into the sea, which thereafter was called the Aegean. (Poem 64)

Aganippe   A spring of the Muses on Mount Helicon. (Poem 61)

Amastris A town situated on the Black Sea. (Poem 4)

Ameana Mamurra's mistress. (Poem 41 and possibly 43)

Ancona An Italian town on the Adriatic. (Poem 36)

Androgeos Son of Minos and Pasiphaë of Crete who was murdered by the Athenians during an athletic contest in Athens. (Poem 64)

Antimachus Greek epic poet of the fifth century B.C. whose works were scorned by Catullus and his coterie of poets. (Poem 95)

Aonia Synonymous with Boeotia. (Poem 61)

Arsinoë Berenice's mother-in-law who was deified before her death. (Poem 66)

Aurelius Friend of Catullus. (Poems 11, 15, 16, 21)

Battus Legendary king of Cyrene in North Africa. (Poem 7)

Berenice Wife of Ptolemy III of Egypt who reigned in the third century B.C. (Poem 66)

Bithynia A Roman Province in Asia Minor. (Poems 10, 25, 31)

Caelius Marcus Caelius Rufus, a well-known politician and orator. (Poems 58, 69, 77, 100)

Caesar Gaius Julius Caesar. (Poems 11, 54, 57, 93)

Callimachus Greek poet of the third century B.C. He was a leader of the Alexandrian school and much admired by Catullus and his poet friends. (Poems 65, 116)

Calvus Gaius Licinius Calvus, celebrated poet friend of Catullus. (Poems 14, 50, 53, 96)

Cato Probably Publius Valerius Cato, older poet friend of Catullus. (Poem 56)

Chalybes A people in Asia Minor who were famous for their production of iron. (Poem 66)

Cicero Marcus Tullius Cicero. There is much disagreement among scholars whether this poem is ironic or not. (Poem 49)

Cinna Gaius Helvius Cinna, poet friend of Catullus. Mistaken for Cinna, one of Caesar's murderers, he was killed following Caesar's death in 44 B.C. (Poems 10, 95, 113)

Cnidus A town in Asia Minor famous for its three temples dedicated to Venus. (Poem 36)

Cornelius Cornelius Nepos, a historian whose lost work, the *Cronica*, Catullus refers to in dedicating his poetry to Nepos in Poem 1. It is not known whether he is the Cornelius who is referred to in Poems 67 or 102.

Cornificius Quintus Cornificius, poet friend of Catullus. (Poem 38)

Cybele The Great Mother Goddess (Magna Mater) whose cult originated in Phrygia (Asia Minor). It was introduced in Greece in the fifth century B.C. and in Rome in 204 B.C. Her rites were accompanied by ecstatic dancing; her priests were obliged to be castrated. (Poems 35, 63)

Cyclades A group of islands in the Aegean Sea. (Poem 4)

Delos An island sacred to Apollo and Diana. (Poem 34)

Dindymus Cybele's sacred mountain in Phrygia (Asia Minor). (Poem 63)

Dyrrachium A port on the east coast of the Adriatic where travelers between Italy and Greece often paused to rest. (Poem 36)

Emathia Synonymous with Thessaly. (Poem 64)

Fabullus A friend of Catullus. (Poems 12, 13, 28, 47)

Furius A friend of Catullus. (Poems 11, 16, 23, 24, 26)

Gallae   Self-castrated priests of Cybele. (Poem 63)

Gellius   One of Lesbia's numerous lovers. (Poems 74, 80, 88, 89, 90, 91, 116)

Golgi   A town on the island of Cyprus where there was a well-known temple of Venus. (Poems 36, 64)

Harpocrates   The Egyptian god Horus, mistakenly regarded by the Greeks and Romans as the god of silence. (Poem 102)

Helicon   A mountain near Mount Parnassus in Boeotia; the home of the Muses. (Poem 61)

Hymen   The god who presides over marriages. (Poems 61, 62, 64)

Hyperboreans   A legendary people who were believed to live in the far north where the sun rose and set only once a year. (Poem 115)

Hyrcania   A barbaric country on the southern shores of the Caspian Sea. (Poem 11)

Ida   A mountain near Troy, sacred to the goddess Cybele. (Poem 63) There is another Mount Ida in Crete. (Poem 64)

Idalium   A town in Cyprus famous for its temple to Venus. (Poems 36, 64)

Juventius   See Introduction, pp. xi, xiii. (Poems 24, 48, 81, 99)

Ladas   A famous runner, courier of Alexander the Great. (Poem 58A)

Lake Larius   Lake Como in Northern Italy. (Poem 35)

Laodamia   Wife of Protesilaus, a Greek who was killed at the beginning of the Trojan War, very shortly after his marriage. (Poem 68A)

Larissa A town in Thessaly. (Poem 64)

Lesbia See Introduction, pp. ix, x, xi, xiii and passim. (Poems 2, 3, 5, 7, 8, 11, 36, 43, 51, 58, 70, 72, 75, 76, 79, 83, 86, 87, 92, 107)

Mamurra Julius Caesar's chief engineer (*Praefectus fabrum*) during the Gallic Wars (59–48 B.C.). Catullus, Cicero, and Horace all refer to his dishonest acquisition of wealth. (Poems 29, 57)

Manlius Lucius Manlius Torquatus was a supporter of Pompey and an enemy of Caesar. He was killed in North Africa in 47 B.C. during the civil wars. (Poems 61, 68)

Memmius Gaius Memmius was propraetor of Bithynia in 57 B.C. He was accompanied to his province by both Catullus and the poet Cinna. He is referred to as "praetor" in Poem 10. Lucretius dedicated his didactic poem *De Rerum Natura* to him. (Poem 28)

Nemesis The goddess who inflicts punishment for wrongdoing. (Poem 50)

Novum Comum A town on the shores of Lake Como. (Poem 35)

Ortalus Quintus Hortensius Hortalus, poet friend of Catullus. (Poem 65 and probably 95)

Parthia A country in Asia hostile to Rome and famed for its archers. (Poem 11)

Peleus King of Thessaly and an Argonaut, the only mortal to be permitted to marry a goddess. He married Thetis, a sea nymph who bore him Achilles. (Poem 64)

Pelion A mountain in Thessaly. (Poem 64)

Peneus A river in Thessaly. (Poem 64)

Pharsalian Adjectival form of *Pharsalus,* a town in Thessaly. (Poem 64)

Phrygia   A country in Asia Minor. (Poems 46, 63, 64)

Piso   Probably Lucius Calpurnius Piso, Caesar's father-in-law. (Poems 28, 47)

Pollio   Gaius Asinius Pollio, distinguished political figure, historian, poet, and associate of Catullus, Caesar, Mark Antony, Horace, and Vergil. His brother Asinius Marrucinus, subject of Catullus' invective, was considerably less distinguished. (Poem 12)

Polyxena   Daughter of King Priam of Troy. She was sacrificed on Achilles' tomb after the fall of Troy. (Poem 64)

Pompey   Gnaeus Pompeius Magnus, Roman general and statesman who vied with his father-in-law, Caesar, for control of the Roman state. He is the "son-in-law" of Poem 29. (Poem 113)

Pontus   A country in Asia Minor. (Poems 4, 29)

Protesilaus   See *Laodamia*.

Pumice stone   A very light, porous, volcanic stone with abrasive qualities. Rough ends of papyrus rolls (books) were rubbed smooth with pumice. It was also commonly used as a depilatory. (Poem 1)

Rhamnusian maid   Identical with *Nemesis*.

Radishes and fish   Certain sexual offenders were punished by the insertion of these objects into the anus. (Poem 15)

Rufus   See *Caelius*.

Saetabis   A town in Spain. (Poems 12, 25)

Scamander   A river near Troy. (Poem 64)

Sileni   Satyrs, attendants of Bacchus. (Poem 64)

Simonides   An early Greek lyric poet. (Poem 38)

Sirmio   A promontory on Lake Benacus (Lago di Garda) where Catullus had a summer home. (Poem 31)

Stymphalian birds   Monstrous, man-eating creatures slain by Hercules. (Poem 68A)

Talasius   The Latin name for Hymen. (Poem 61)

Taurus   A mountain range in Asia Minor. (Poem 64)

Tethys   Goddess of the sea, wife of Ocean. (Poems 64, 66, 88)

Themis   Goddess of Justice. (Poem 68A)

Thetis   See *Peleus*.

Tiburtine   Adjectival form of Tibur, modern Tivoli, which is and was a fashionable resort town near Rome. (Poem 39)

Torquatus   See *Manlius*.

Urania   The Muse of Astronomy. (Poem 61)

Urii   A town on Italy's "heel." (Poem 36)

Varus   Quintilius Varus, poetic critic and friend of Catullus. (Poems 10, 22)

Vatinius   Publius Vatinius, political figure, friend of Caesar. (Poems 14, 52, 53)

Veranius   A close friend of Catullus. (Poems 12, 28, 47)

INDEX OF LATIN FIRST LINES

INDEX OF ENGLISH FIRST LINES